WARNING:

The Fig Tree Has Sprouted

How to recognize the signs of the times

Leon Gosiewski

Onwards and Upwards Publishers

Berkeley House, 11 Nightingale Crescent, Leatherhead,
Surrey, KT24 6PD.
www.onwardsandupwards.org

Printed in the UK.

ISBN: 978-1-907509-76-6
Typeface: Sabon LT

Unless stated otherwise, scripture quotations are from the Revised Standard Version of the Bible, copyright © 1946, 1952, and 1971 the Division of Christian Education of the National Council of the Churches of Christ in the United States of America. Used by permission. All rights reserved.

Scripture quotations marked (NIV) are from THE HOLY BIBLE, NEW INTERNATIONAL VERSION®, NIV® Copyright © 1973, 1978, 1984, 2011 by Biblica, Inc.™ Used by permission. All rights reserved worldwide.

Scripture quotations marked (NLT) are taken from the Holy Bible, New Living Translation, copyright © 1996, 2004, 2007 by Tyndale House Foundation. Used by permission of Tyndale House Publishers, Inc., Carol Stream, Illinois 60188. All rights reserved.

Scripture quotation marked (KJV) are taken from the King James Version of the Bible.

Scripture marked (NASB) taken from the NEW AMERICAN STANDARD BIBLE®, Copyright © 1960, 1962, 1963, 1968, 1971, 1972, 1973, 1975, 1977, 1995 by The Lockman Foundation. Used by permission.

"Blow the trumpet in Zion; sound the alarm on my holy mountain! Let all the inhabitants of the land tremble, for the day of the LORD is coming, it is near, a day of darkness and gloom, a day of clouds and thick darkness! Like blackness there is spread upon the mountains a great and powerful people; their like has never been from of old, nor will be again after them through the years of all generations. Fire devours before them, and behind them a flame burns. The land is like the Garden of Eden before them, but after them a desolate wilderness, and nothing escapes them." (Joel 2:1-3)

Endorsements

Boldly shedding the reluctance, or even the fear, many of us have regarding end times, Leon approaches Bible prophecy carefully, scripturally, and historically. The author reminds us that the very one who admonishes us to be alert is the same Christ to whom we are to point others to likewise be prepared. This is a timely, relevant, and effective tool for every Christian who genuinely desires to walk in the light, just as Jesus is in the light.

John W. Styles, Ph. D.
International Speaker and Author[1]

Leon Gosiewski writes on a subject vital to Christians everywhere. In these closing days of time, once again a trumpet sound is being heard, preparing the Church for the return of Jesus, their Messiah, Saviour and King.

Leon does not claim any great academic background or deep theological study. He writes from his heart and from a lifelong experience of listening to the Holy Spirit. Based on Biblical prophecy he points out the fact of the Second Coming and passionately challenges us to be ready.

Having had the privilege of meeting face to face with Leon, and discovering his true heart and passion, I unreservedly recommend this book to all believers.

Dr Tony Stone
International Evangelist

---

[1] *All the Damn Christians: A Glimpse into the Mirror of Hypocrisy;* published by Sonfire Media

Leon is a writer of excellence and spiritual depths, yet to the layman easy to grasp. He has captured deep scriptural truths on the prophets of both old and present day. This is a must read that will bring deep understanding regarding end times as we wait for the inevitable return of Christ.

Peter Gladwin
Author[2], International Speaker and Evangelist

This publication by Leon Gosiewski is just one of a series of excellent books he has written. I am well acquainted with Leon's fervour to stir up the body of Christ by scholarly research and inspired writing, and he has without doubt done this here.

Leon has a powerful testimony of his own, and what he writes has been drawn from many years of Christian experience and his passion for the truth of Holy Scripture.

Leon, in writing this book, tackles the dangers most of us fall into at some stage of our faith, the necessity of having our hearts enlightened to biblical truth. His style of writing is simple and straightforward, yet covers important issues with such reassuring biblical detail.

This is a very readable book and will be a valuable resource for all thinking and sensitive Christians and all those who desire to reach maturity in their faith.

Difficult questions require simple solutions and those are found in such books as this one. We therefore need very much authors like Leon to clearly face up to the challenges that are expressed in this publication.

I would therefore thoroughly recommend this book and the others Leon Gosiewski has written for he has done an outstanding job.

Barrie Stevens
Evangelist and International Speaker

---

[2] *Out of the Ashes;* published by Lion Hudson

About the Author

Leon Gosiewski is the founder of *Renewed Life Healing* and *Chasing Your Dreams* community ministries.

Qualified to Master of Science degree with further credentials in sport psychology, counselling and education, Leon also undertook training in Old and New Testament studies, church history and pastoral care.

Leon has spent over thirty years in sport and fitness education. Having witnessed the healing touch of God and lived a number of years in the 'wilderness', Leon has sought answers to a number of faith questions. Leon does not shirk or hide from hard, scrutinising questions, not least of which are "How can negativity be replaced with positivity in our lives?" "What has happened to everyday healing miracles?" and "Where has the power gone to attain our dreams?"

Through faith in God combined with caring and compassionate teaching *Chasing Your Dreams* and *Renewed Life Healing* ministries help to remove blocks that prevent people from achieving their healing needs and unlocking their potential to walk in the supernatural lifestyle that God intends.

About 'Chasing Your Dreams'

In partnership with *Renewed Life Healing* ministries, *Chasing Your Dreams* is a unique international healing and teaching organization.

God's mandate on this ministry is to "open the eyes that are blind... bring out the prisoners from the dungeon, from the prison those who sit in darkness" (Isaiah 42:6,7) and to set captives free. The calling of this ministry is to heal the church. Part of this healing involves stirring the church to prepare for the second coming and to be ready.

Many churches are not preparing their congregations about what it means to be ready. Sadly, because of this many may become like the foolish maidens who could have participated in the wedding feast but were not fully prepared and ready when the moment arrived.[3]

---

[3] Matthew 25:1-13

Prayer

May the Holy Spirit take these words and use this publication to lift and revive those who enter these pages, not as a substitute for the scriptures (for these can never be substituted) but to inspire greater commitment to Your word. I pray that the Spirit of revival will be globally released in mighty power upon those who set their hearts on You to open blind eyes, set captives free and bring light where there was darkness – and may the Lord's name be glorified.

Lord God, I believe that you are true to your word, and therefore you will touch and bless all those who read this book.

Author's Note

In my last book[4] I said:

My heart cries in anguish to have the words to adequately share with you my feelings about the depths to which Satan has deceived many Christian believers and to show afresh the true heart and will of God. God is calling and stirring His chosen ones to prepare for an outpouring of His Spirit and for battle. As an individual and collectively as the church we cannot continue to live as we are.

This is a time like no other. The Bible warns us to watchfully prepare. Perhaps nowhere is this better summed up than in these words:

Luke 21: 35
Watch at all times, praying that you have strength to escape all these things that will take place, and to stand before the Son of man.

Dear reader, something supernatural is stirring. The final countdown call for the bride of Christ to watch the signs and be ready is sounded. It is a call of preparation; to 'leave no stone unturned' so that our eternal salvation is firm and secure. It is a call to walk in holiness, filled with the Holy Spirit and supernaturally equipped.

The need to be watchful and faithful was the clear exhortation of Jesus in Matthew 24:36-51 where He said, "Watch therefore" (verse 42) and "be ready" (verse 44).

Just as Noah warned the people, so there will be plenty of warnings. There will be an increase of God's messengers bringing warning messages. The last pieces of the jigsaw are being put in place before Christ returns.

As a prophetic statement, it is my conviction that we will see many of God's chosen people ready and walking in a new and invigorated way with Him, a supernatural way. It will also see many

---

[4] *The Language of Knowing Our Heavenly Father's Heart and Will;* published by Onwards and Upwards Publishers

others losing their way, compromising their faith and even falling away from God. A number who fall into this trap will do so without realising it at first; it will come by stealth. Apathy, complacency and settling for second best will mean that many will miss out. Our destiny awaits.

Smith Wigglesworth once said, "If I leave you as I found you, I am not God's channel." I fear with godly fear to say it, but if this book leaves you as it found you I have not written as a channel of God.

Explanatory Note

The term 'Jew' is not used in this book unless it is directly taken from scripture verses quoted. This decision is out of respect for a people who have suffered much and in humble recognition of the fact that this term has been (and is) often used in a derogatory and derisory nature.

Acknowledgements

Expressing my love for Jesus is difficult to put into words, but without Him I am nothing but a sinner and lost soul.

With heartfelt thanks to those nearest to my heart whom I love deeply and who in return love me, forgive me and show so much patience toward me.

With thanks to Chrissy.

Leon Gosiewski
March 2013

All glory and praise are given to God who has never failed me or forsaken me even though I have repeatedly failed Him. In thanks, I offer myself as a living sacrifice.

Contents

Warning: The Fig Tree Has Sprouted

Preface

No, this is not a gardening book in the sense that those interested in arboriculture, botany, floriculture or horticulture would understand. It is also not a book suggesting fig trees have some sort of power that we should receive warnings about. This book is however about planting, nurturing and cultivating the seed of the word of God firmly in our spirit, heart and mind. It is a warning reminder that carries a spiritual health check. It sounds a tsunami type siren that life events and distractions will imminently overtake many; sweeping the unexpected and unrepentant away in a tidal wave of procrastination, apathy, complacency and indifference.

Those left standing – the humble, hungry and thirsty – will receive signs and supernatural power. They will know the message that was given to the church in Philadelphia, which says, "I have set before you an open door, which no one is able to shut; I know that you have but little power, and yet you have kept my word and have not denied my name" (Revelation 3: 8). An open door to the heart of heaven will stay unfastened to those who will go deeper with God.

The message of this book is simple and yet the most important of our lives. It is about watching for God's end-time harvest and being fully prepared and equipped.

The importance of the following questions cannot be over-emphasized:

- Why does the Bible place so much emphasis on being ready?
- Why did Jesus make a particular point about ensuring we are ready?

If there is one message contained in this book that is more important than any other, it is that every Christian believer puts themselves in a state of readiness and alertness.

This book does not claim any particular specialist background. Led by the Holy Spirit, the perspective of this book finds its focus in the Christian experience, research and passion for biblical truth of a Gentile Christian believer.

Lessons from God's chosen people and prophecies of the Old Testament are carefully integrated with a Christian's New Testament faith in Jesus and longing to go deeper with God.

This is a call to carry our lamps and have spare oil.

Prologue

In my first two books I began with prophecy statements that I will abridge here because of their impending importance:

> *Yet once more I will shake not only the earth but also the heavens. There is coming a fresh wave of God's power and we are right now at the very brink, the start of this revival that will outstretch any other revival.*

This book begins with understanding Bible prophecy because prophecy forms a sizeable part of the scriptures. On over two thousand four hundred and eighty occasions we read phrases such as "I will", "in that day", "it shall", "the Lord said". We also have about eighteen hundred references to the second coming and the end of the age. With this in mind it must surely be vitally important that we understand what prophecy is and know how to rightly handle the word of God. After all, it is through prophecy that our fears, uncertainties and misunderstandings are soothingly quelled; allowing us to build our faith and strengthen our relationship with God as His plans are openly revealed.

Although a significant proportion of the Bible is prophecy, many churches surprisingly neglect its study, misunderstand its importance, and even go as far as despising the prophets. Peter writes:

2 Peter 1:19
We have the prophetic word made more sure. You will do well to pay attention to this as to a lamp shining in a dark place, until the day dawns and the morning star rises in your hearts.

It is to our grave cost that we do not understand, pay attention to and obey God's revelations.

The heart of God toward Israel is clearly expressed through His promise to honour Israel and bring salvation:

Isaiah 62:1
For Zion's sake I will not be silent, and for Jerusalem's sake I will not rest, until her vindication goes forth as brightness, and her salvation as a burning torch.

God intends to bring spiritual renewal to Israel (see Romans 11:25-32); it is also his purpose that Jewish and Christian believers alike would guard against the clever deceptions and plausibly presented false teachings that would try to separate those whom God loves.

The twenty-first century has begun to see increasing fulfillment of God's end time purpose for Jewish people and Christian alike in a way and at a speed not seen before. This is a purpose that has an impact on all nations and the destiny of humankind.

For far too long the Christian church has ignored the vital importance of God's chosen people and many of the God-given and inspired customs, celebrations and worship. We are the poorer for missing the richness of our heritage and what God has and is doing.

The growing trend toward having Gentile Christian believers' eyes focused toward Israel and the peace of Jerusalem is gathering pace. But much more needs to be done. The main bulk of this book will uncover why every Christian and the Christian church needs to know more about the Jewish people and what God is doing in Israel.

I acknowledge that many foundational theological beliefs are being actively introduced in these last days. Increasingly, however, people are attempting to explain scripture through their fallible understanding and with the aim to promote and satisfy their own beliefs. In another words, some are trying to explain what they do not feel comfortable with (or understand) by using their own intellect, manipulating scripture instead of seeking the Holy Spirit for guidance. Writing to Timothy, Paul put this point as follows:

> 2 Timothy 4:3,4
> *People will not endure sound teaching, but having itching ears they will accumulate for themselves teachers to suit their own likings, and will turn away from listening to the truth and wander into myths.*

As we progress through this book we will tackle the inclusive truth of God's loving heart and promises to both Jewish and Gentile people. We will also uncover the holy love welling up and gathering pace between the Jewish believers and Gentiles. A love that is breaking down what were originally wounds of hatred that are so old many of us do not really understand what it was all about.

Those who wish to engage in these arguments may have a place but great care needs to be taken, keeping these words in mind:

Philippians 2:3,4

Do nothing from selfishness or conceit, but in humility count others better than yourselves. Let each of you look not only to his own interests, but also to the interests of others.

This book does not seek to enter speculative theological debate or ally itself with any particular man-inspired agenda, sect or movement. Rather it is firmly based upon bringing the Spirit and Word together. I cannot express my point in any better way than through the inimitable words of Smith Wigglesworth who said:

Some people like to read their Bibles in the Hebrew; some like to read it in the Greek; I like to read it in the Holy Spirit.[5]

It is not easy to admit, but we have generally grown dull in our understanding of God's purposes because the cares of this world, our disobedience, ego, unbelief and faithlessness have blinded our eyes and spiritual sensitivity. If only we would turn our focus back to God in humility and sacrifice of self we could once again have our eyes opened and our misunderstandings clarified.

When Jesus spoke with the Samaritan woman He crossed the barriers that had existed between Jewish and non-Jewish people. Jesus then spoke these words:

John 4:21-24

The hour is coming when neither on this mountain nor in Jerusalem will you worship the Father. You worship what you do not know; we worship what we know, for salvation is from the Jews. But the hour is coming, and now is, when the true worshippers will worship the Father in spirit and truth, for such the Father seeks to worship him. God is spirit, and those who worship him must worship in spirit and truth.

Jesus reminds us that we must not forget "salvation is from the Jews". True worshippers worship in spirit and truth.

---

[5] *www.mybiblequotes.com/smith-wigglesworth-quotes*

How to read this book

This book is not a substitute for the Bible. Guidance of the Holy Spirit has been sought in writing the chapters as a spur to encourage those who enter these pages and motivate them to read more of God's word. It claims no more than this.

Each chapter is specifically written in a way that requires prayerful reading, seeking direction from the Holy Spirit, our Counsellor and Teacher. It is for this reason that all the chapters begin with an introductory scripture verse and a 'seed thought'. A little time to contemplate these should be taken before reading the chapter.

Every chapter consists of scripture references, and it is these that should bring the reader to seek the truth of what God is saying and encourage deeper research of the Bible.

Chapter outlines

Jesus prophetically warned that false prophets would come in the last days. There will be those preaching a diluted gospel message, and some will preach plausible messages or create new theological beliefs that are contrary to scripture. Many will listen to these messages and their heads will be turned both subtly and blatantly from God's truth.

Chapter one seeks to understand Bible prophecy, the prophets and why their messages are important. We learn how to recognize the prophetic word and why despising it and the messenger displeases God.

Chapter two naturally links prophecy with knowing and understanding the prophetic signs. Many of us want to know if Jesus will return in our lifetime. For others this question is pushed to the back of their thinking either through fear or lack of teaching.

The truth is none of us know when this will happen. Our duty is simply to keep alert, be ready and live each day as if Jesus is about to appear. The danger we must avoid is to live as if Jesus is not coming back in our lifetime and so find ourselves 'soft' targets for deception and unprepared like the five foolish maidens.

We live in an age when God's prophetic words are supernaturally being revealed in front of our eyes. Jesus encouraged us to watch for the signs and so here we look at what these signs are and how we should react to them. This chapter not only encourages the reader to look for the signs but also to prepare for the return of Jesus. It is a warning not to become complacent or to get caught up in misguided teaching, philosophy, theology, denominationalism or precepts of men.

As we consider the prophecies and signs pointing to the close of the age **chapter three** turns our attention to Jerusalem, God's chosen center of focus, His holy city. In this chapter we consider what it means to pray for the peace of Jerusalem. During the course of this chapter we will investigate why Jerusalem is so important, and we will also take a brief tour of the ups and downs of this beautiful, vibrant ancient city.

We could not talk about Jerusalem without saying something about the building of the third temple, and so the closing section is given to briefly discussing this topic.

For some the building of the third temple is controversial and for others emotionally highly charged. This, along with revelations of the first two chapters, leads us into **chapter four** and the highly significant end time battle: Gog and Magog.

Ancient prophecies about the last day's attack on Israel are in some ways descriptively detailed and in others tantalizingly unclear. There is a balance that I hope this book will highlight. Namely, there are things that God has revealed, and He expects us to pay heed to them; and there are things God has either not revealed or only partially revealed, but He expects us to have faith in Him and trust Him.

As we come to **chapter five** it might appear that we go 'off on a tangent' as we spend time looking at God's holy convocations. However, the relevance of the chapter will be explained as the teaching unfolds.

We discover that the foundations of the Christian faith are found in Jewish life and their Hebraic culture. The church has a Hebrew heritage; however, many Christians have little or no understanding of their roots because relations between the Church and Jewish people were sadly broken. Just as many of us have a deep longing to know about our ancestry and genealogy so we should know about our spiritual ancestry. These give us a sense of belonging, knowledge and understanding of who we are and how we fit in.

During the course of this chapter we will learn that we are living in the emblematic latter-day summer harvest. We are serving God and working in the 'fields' or, as Jesus said to Simon and Andrew, we are "fishers of men" (Mark 1:17), gathering the end time harvest of souls.

As we learn more about our heritage and who the Jewish Jesus was, we also place this into the context of the new covenant. We will discover that with our freedom comes a responsibility to walk in humility, love and holiness.

Many questions arise from these five opening chapters. Not least of these is the vital question of our readiness to meet Jesus. **Chapter six** gives us the opportunity to explore what we need to do to get ready for Him. It is here where we will come to the fullness of understanding these words:

> **Hebrews 9:28**
> *So Christ, having been offered once to bear the sins of many, will appear a second time, not to deal with sin but to save those who are eagerly waiting for him.*

The question here is: are we eagerly waiting for Jesus, and are we preparing ourselves for our bridegroom? Jesus is coming for those who are "eagerly waiting for him".

We complete this book by looking again at our faith and beliefs. Here we are shamelessly challenged to renew our walk in a way that will cause us to become lights in a dark world; to live in such a way that every day is a supernatural day.

It is one thing to quote scripture and quite another to live by it. Unbelief is our greatest hindrance to releasing God's power. Many of the children of Israel did not enter the Promised Land because of their unbelief. The challenge of this final chapter is to 'walk the talk' and not 'talk the walk'.

Our very lives should radiate Jesus. In the book of Proverbs we read:

> **Proverbs 16:24**
> *Pleasant words are like a honeycomb, sweetness to the soul and health to the body.*

Our bodies should display wholesomeness, and our words like honey should draw others to God through us.

The concluding section of this book is a contextual overview. It looks at the traditional Jewish marriage ceremony. Here we not only see everything covered in this book in perspective but also come face to face with what being the bride of Christ truly means.

Revelation 19:7,8
Let us rejoice and exult and give him the glory, for the marriage of the Lamb has come, and his Bride has made herself ready; it was granted her to be clothed with fine linen, bright and pure – for the fine linen is the righteous deeds of the saints.

Warning: The Fig Tree Has Sprouted

CHAPTER ONE

Understanding Bible Prophecy

1 Thessalonians 5:19-22
Do not quench the Spirit, do not despise prophesying, but test everything; hold fast what is good, abstain from every form of evil.

Seed thought

You have to take Bible prophecy literally, just like everything else in the Bible.

- Tim LaHaye[6]

Introduction

Many Christians have tragically grown to only pay lip service to (or even for the most part ignore) prophecy. They misunderstand its relevance, and some even go as far as to despise it. As a result of these attitudes most fail to study what it is actually about, and some even say that the prophet's office is no longer relevant. Taking to heart or believing any of these statements is not only biblically incorrect but also contrary to the true Christian's relationship with God.

In the New Testament book of Revelation we read that "the testimony of Jesus is the spirit of prophecy" (Revelation 19:10). If this is true then surely we cannot afford to do anything else but take heed to it because it is an indispensable part of our day-by-day relational living. The gospel message itself is not just about Jesus, the

---

[6] *www.brainyquote.com/quotes/quotes/t/timlahaye240816.html*

cross, love, faith and belief. It is a prophetic message that carries with it the end time assurance or guarantee of eternal life in the kingdom of God.

At the beginning of the book of Revelation we read:

Revelation 1:3
Blessed is he who reads aloud the words of the prophecy, and blessed are those who hear, and who keep what is written therein; for the time is near.

The closing chapter of Revelation then says:

Revelation 22:10
Do not seal up the words of the prophecy of this book, for the time is near.

How can anyone say that prophecy has no relevance today? Prophecy reveals God's plans; it provides warnings and it tells us of future events. It helps us to understand God's purposes and ways. It is also a message from God that we should heed and obey. For example, many scriptures in the Old Testament foretold the events of the New Testament and in particular the coming of Jesus. Several prophecies from both Testaments point to God's end time plans.

As we move ahead through this chapter many of these opening thoughts will begin to take shape and meaning; therefore let's discover the vital place of prophecy and identify the pitfalls of misrepresenting its God-intended significance.

Background

It has probably not escaped your attention that the title of this book refers to the sprouting fig tree. What then has this opening chapter on understanding Bible prophecy got to do with the fig tree? And what, in any case, is the fig tree all about?

Jesus, following His prophetic 'Mount of Olives' statements recorded in Matthew 24, Mark 13 and Luke 21, suddenly appears to go off on a tangent and introduces the parable of the fig tree. This unexpected divergence prompts us to ask, why does Jesus suddenly introduce a parable amidst prophecy?

In order to appreciate what was behind the thoughts of Jesus at this point of the conversation let's first check what a parable is. The Greek word for parable is *parabole* meaning 'to place one thing beside another, juxtaposition, comparison, similitude' or, to place this in its biblical context, 'an earthly story conveying a heavenly meaning'. The Hebrew word is *mashal* meaning 'to represent, to compare or be like'. Today we might call this an allegory.

Not only was Jesus foretelling a series of future events, but also He was crucially explaining that these events have a deeply significant and heavenly purpose – a purpose that we must take heed of, look out for and act upon. You see, the context that underpins why Jesus introduced a parable at this stage of the conversation is that having made a number of important prophetic statements during the question-and-answer discourse with His disciples, Jesus wanted to make sure that His disciples (and each of us because the prophecies have not all been fully fulfilled yet) would look out for and take heed of the outworking of the prophetic statements. Jesus was, if you like, urging the vital importance of watching and being ready.

Why? Because they represent significant heavenly warning signs that humanity can refer to and see God's tangible hand at work. To ignore these signs is not only to ignore God but foolishness of epic proportions. The church has for far too long downplayed prophecy, and it does so at its own cost. Evidence in scripture shows that where prophecy is totally ignored it has stirred God's wrath and landed many in deep trouble.

To put this point in another way, Jesus wanted to prevent us from falling into the trap that many throughout scripture and history have fallen into: the costly trap of taking a supercilious approach to the prophetic word and ignoring God's warnings. He was seeking to show that God does not want us ignorant of what is to come and why these things will take place. He wants us fully prepared and ready.

Prepared and ready for what exactly? What am I talking about? Jesus explained with the following words:

Matthew 24:37-39

As was the days of Noah, so will be the coming of the Son of man. For as in those days before the flood they were eating and drinking, marrying and giving in marriage, until the day when Noah entered the ark, and they did not know until the flood came and swept them all away.

We must be fully ready, fully equipped, fully in tune with God and not caught sleeping, procrastinating and sitting with our 'spiritual feet' up in ineffectiveness. Noah gave more than fair and adequate warning to the people, but they would not listen.

We do not know how long it took Noah to build the ark other than it was built between his five hundredth and six hundredth birthdays. What we do know is it must have taken several years, and when the door of the ark closed and the blue skies suddenly turned black and rain fell it was too late for the people who had not taken heed of the prophetic warnings.

No one in the days of Noah could say that they were not told or they did not know. No one today can say that they were not told or they did not know. In actual fact, today we have less of an excuse than those in Noah's day. We have the benefit of seeing what happened to them!

In order to grasp the crucial importance of what Jesus was trying to convey through this parable, let's take a closer look at what He said.

> **Matthew 24:32,33; Mark 13:28,29**
> *From the fig tree learn its lesson: as soon as its branch becomes tender and puts forth its leaves, you know that summer is near. So also, when you see all these things, you know that he is near, at the very gates.*

If we truly know that Jesus is near and at the gates, are we going to sit still? Are we going to shrug our shoulders and say, "I've heard that one before"? Or are we going to run eagerly to meet him?

> **Luke 21:29-31**
> *Look at the fig tree, and all the trees; as soon as they come out in leaf, you see for yourselves and know that the summer is already near. So also, when you see these things taking place, you know that the kingdom of God is near.*

If we know that the kingdom of God is near it should stir us to action. Procrastination and complacency are two of the biggest robbers to strike humanity and in particular the Christian believer. They rob what otherwise God longs to give. Procrastination and complacency mixed with humanism is destroying the effectiveness of the church and weakening Christian believers who feed on a diet of 'junk' that leads to spiritually malnourished growth.

I cannot reiterate the message too many times. Having declared a series of prophetic statements leading up to this parable, what Jesus was saying is that just as we know the signs of approaching seasons so we should know and look for God's prophetic signs and be forewarned. These are indicators that the kingdom of God is at hand. The end of the age is close.

We have and are seeing these prophecies fulfilled. We live in a generation where we can historically see how God has foretold future events and given warnings. We are seeing prophecies being fulfilled in front of our very eyes. And we are probably better placed today than any generation before us to look backward and forwards in time and interpret Bible prophecy.

The fig tree has sprouted! We are living in an age of prophetic revelation. The prophecies that Jesus left us with enable believers to peek into the future. The world we live in is being undeniably shaken. It is being 'turned upside-down' with disasters, floods, economic struggles, wars and famines. People are turning their backs on God, and terrible atrocities hit our headlines almost daily. Yes, it is true that these are not new. But the intensity and scale of them is different; they are global. All of this is clearly prophesied in scripture, and so we can look at these awful events and know that God forewarned us that our pride and sinful nature would produce its outcome. God will, however, have the last say. He will bring those that are true to Him into 'the ark' of safety, and He will cut the wicked and unrepentant off.

The 'love gospel'[7] advocates will not want to accept my last comment. But the facts are plain for us to see. An end will come. Choices will have ultimately been made by each of us. I do not want to leave anything to chance. I would rather respond like Joshua:

> Joshua 24:15
> *If you be unwilling to serve the Lord, choose this day whom you will serve, whether the gods your father served in the region beyond the River, or the gods of the Amorites in whose land you dwell; but as for me and my household, we will serve the Lord.*

In light of what we are beginning to unravel, the parable of Jesus about the fig tree takes on a new perspective and, of course, sounds

---

[7] See Appendix II.

like (and is) very good advice. Surely, therefore, it would be foolhardy for the godly to sit back and remain inactive and unprepared. And worse still, to fight and squabble among one another; to place more emphasis on doctrine and tradition than God's word!

I started writing this book in 2011, though the main part was written in 2012. I am nonetheless totally convinced that throughout 2013 we will see and hear an increasing number of warnings from prophets and preachers across the world. But how can we truly recognize, understand and be on familiar terms with God's prophecy? And what are these prophecies we are talking about anyway?

How can we recognize biblical prophecy?

Before we can begin to recognize, appreciate and understand prophecy it will prove useful and necessary to understand what it is. Armed with this thought, and beginning with the Collins dictionary, I was particularly intrigued to discover that it defines prophecy as:

> *A message of divine truth revealing God's will, the act of uttering such a message, a prediction or guess, the charismatic endowment of a prophet.*[8]

At first glance this looked very good. What we are talking about here are clearly predicted or foretold messages from God communicated to a chosen prophet whose role is to proclaim them to others. Great! But I soon realized that to stop here would be both unwise and misleading. So let's investigate this definition a little deeper and unpack the shortcomings of what the dictionary has to say.

If we look at the same dictionary's definition of a prophet we find this description:

> *A person who speaks by divine inspiration. One through whom a divinity expresses his will, a person who predicts the future or a spokesman for a movement or doctrine.*[9]

---

[8] Reproduced from Collins English Dictionary and Thesaurus with the permission of HarperCollins Publishers Ltd. © HarperCollins Publishers 1990. Collins ® is a registered trademark of HarperCollins Publishers Ltd. Collins English Dictionary and Thesaurus (1990) ISBN 9780004331869

[9] Ibid.

By combining these two definitions we discover that not all is as it might seem.

The added inclusion of the word 'guess' in the 'prophecy' definition suggests not all prophecy is divine or of God because by definition God does not guess. He is all knowing; He knows what is going to happen. The uniqueness of Bible prophecy is its specificity, preciseness and proven fulfilled accuracy.

A further point to consider is the term 'divine truth'. Prophecy that proves by outcome to be inaccurate or wrong, such as "the world will end on such-and-such a date" cannot be divine truth. It cannot be divinely inspired.

Why? First there have been many such predictions in every century since the early church. All of which have obviously been wrong. Also the Bible actually says, "No one knows, not even the angels of heaven, nor the Son, but the Father only" (Matthew 24:36). Be ready, yes. But pay no attention to those who spread such rumours. God is not going to divinely tell anyone!

As we look at the definitions of a prophet further questions arise as follows:

- *"Through whom a divinity expresses his will."* This is now going beyond God and includes religious divinities, gods or deities.
- *"A person who predicts the future."* Clearly God has now been taken out of the equation and a person is predicting and speaking on his or her own behalf.
- *"A spokesperson for a movement or doctrine."* Again here this person is not speaking the words given to them directly by God, who is outside the realms of a human movement or artificial doctrine.

What has been starkly unveiled here is that there is a marked difference between biblical prophecy – God's prophetic word and those chosen by God as His prophets – and other forms of prophecy. There are prophets associated with prophecy that is totally unconnected to God. Indeed, when going back to scripture we discover that Jesus was a little more forthright and warned that we must test for false prophets saying, "Beware of false prophets" (Matthew 7:15). The Greek translation here is, *"Prosecho apo pseudoprphetes,"* meaning, "Give heed (or beware) of one who is acting the part of a divinely inspired prophet."

It is clear then that a God-inspired prophet is a person who speaks to an individual, to groups or even to entire nations the words of a message received directly from Him. Thus a Bible or Christian believer prophet is someone who has God-given authority to speak the words that He has given to them on His behalf. This point is perhaps clearly expressed for us by Amos who said:

> **Amos 3:7**
> *Surely the Lord God does nothing, without revealing his secret to his servants the prophets.*

When we look at the Hebrew word 'to prophesy' we find the word *naba* meaning 'to speak or even to sing by inspiration or by influence of a divine spirit'. God reveals His secrets, and He does so through those in whom He can trust.

In order to understand a little more about who or what a prophet is, let's take a closer look at the best source of information available to us and what the Bible has to say. The Old Testament Hebrew word for prophet is *nabi* or *nabiy* and the New Testament Greek word is *profetes* from which the English word 'prophet' derives.

Nabiy: This is the most often used word to describe a prophet. It means 'to bubble up, be stirred to declare, to utter, a spokesperson or speaker'.

Two other words are also found in the Old Testament to describe a prophet. The prophet Samuel was described by the Hebrew word *roeh,* and King David's prophet Gad was similarly described with the word *chozeh.*

Roeh, chozeh: Both of these words mean 'a seer' or 'a person who sees'. An example of the term *roeh* is found in the following:

> **1 Samuel 9:8-10**
> *The servant answered Saul again, 'Here, I have with me the fourth part of a shekel of silver, and I will give it to the man of God, to tell us our way.' (Formerly in Israel, when a man went to inquire of God, he said, 'Come, let us go to the seer'; for he who is now called a prophet was formerly called a seer). And Saul said to his servant, 'Well said; come, let us go.' So they went to the city where the man of God was.*

In 1 Chronicles 29: 29 all three Hebrew words are used:

Now the acts of King David, from first to last, are written in the Chronicles of Samuel the seer [roeh], and in the chronicles of Nathan the prophet [nabiy], and in the Chronicles of Gad the seer [chozeh].

The original Hebrew text reads:

Dabar melek David rishown acharown kathab dabar shemuwel roeh dabar Nathan nabiy debar Gad chozeh.

It is a wonderful fact that in His mercy and grace God foretells and warns us of things to come or of consequences of our actions, and so on. This fact is clear in scripture from beginning to end. The bedrock of scripture is God's communication with humanity, which does not listen and does not learn. There are many examples of this including the following from Isaiah:

Isaiah 42:9
Behold, the former things have come to pass, and new things I now declare; before they spring forth I tell you of them.

The characteristic trait of God is to keep us informed. There are no hidden messages tucked away in the 'small print'. We are not left to guess. We have no excuse and that is why Jesus again said that we should "from the fig tree learn its lesson" (Matthew 24:32).

Due to concerned implications of mysticism there are those who will understandably say that the prophecy of a God-inspired prophet is not about foretelling but rather about 'forth telling'. This can often be a little confusing because in the process of forth telling a word from God the message can include foretelling something that is to happen. The point that needs fully grasping is that biblical prophets are not mystics or fortune-tellers. They claim nothing of themselves but are totally open to God. They speak the words given to them by God. These words may deal with immediate situations, point out sin, lead in certain directions; or they may contain a message of warning and future events. The prophet in this sense may both forth tell and foretell.

In order to illustrate what I mean, God declared these words through the prophet Isaiah:

Isaiah 48:3-5
The former things I declared of old, they went forth from my mouth and I made them known; then suddenly I did them and

33

they came to pass. Because I know that you are obstinate, and your neck is an iron sinew and your forehead brass, I declared them to you from of old, before they came to pass I announced them to you, lest you should say, 'My idol did them, my graven image and my molten image commanded them.'

The prophet is being used as God's mouthpiece. In his second letter Peter helps us to understand these points by saying, "No prophecy ever came by the impulse of man, but men moved by the Holy Spirit spoke from God" (2 Peter 1:21).

A true prophet of God will always point toward God and bring glory to His name. The true prophet will never glorify themselves in any way or speak contrary to God's word. These points help us to understand the difference between those who speak under the anointing of the Holy Spirit and those that speak without the anointing (including those who are outright false prophets – who claim ability to foretell and direct focus *away* from God).

But why does God use a prophet or prophetess to convey His messages?

Why prophets?

When we look back at the Garden of Eden we discover what the natural order of life should really be. Adam and Eve communicated directly with God. It was a face-to-face, interpersonal relationship. This was God's original relational intention for each of us. Sadly sin ruined the relationship between man and God and we read:

Genesis 3:8
The man and his wife hid themselves from the presence of the Lord God among the trees of the garden.

The very first step of breaking relationship with God was actually taken by humanity. Isaiah explained the change of relationship between man and God in these words:

Isaiah 59:2
Your iniquities have made a separation between you and your God, and your sins have hid his face from you so that he does not hear.

Sin raised a barrier between man and God. Incidentally, as we will see later, sin is what raises a barrier of denial when it comes to prophecy.

Although Adam and Eve were summarily expelled from the Garden of Eden and sin to this day separates us from God, an amazing thing happened. God did not give up on man. God found ways of communicating with people whether through dreams, angel visitations, through a person's conscience or through those whom He could trust – the prophets, such as Noah, Abraham, Moses, Miriam, Elijah, Jonah, Anna and many others.

The reason why God uses prophets is clearly explained for us in Deuteronomy 18:15-22. The background to the promise described there came amidst the sin of divination. Since man lost direct communication with God, an appetite to know the future (to know what would happen) led to ungodly practices. God promised to use prophets to speak His words saying:

Deuteronomy 18:18

I will raise up for them a prophet like you [Moses] from among their brethren; and I will put my words in his mouth, and he shall speak to them all that I command him.

Strangely, when we hear something we do not like, we ignore it or brush it to one side. This promise came with a warning:

Deuteronomy 18:19

Whoever will not give heed to my words which he shall speak in my name, I myself will require it of him.

Prophecy is no game. It is not something we can ignore or despise. It must be carefully heeded, otherwise we are answerable directly to God.

God tries to communicate with man individually, but from the beginning (and sadly to this day) we are often 'deaf' because of our sin. It is time to re-think our place; therefore, let's take a moment to seriously consider this scripture:

2 Chronicles 36:15,16

The Lord, the God of their fathers, sent persistently to them by his messengers, because he had compassion on his people and on his dwelling place; but they kept mocking the messengers of God, despising his words, and scoffing at his prophets, till the wrath of the Lord rose against his people, till there was no remedy.

When we see this wish to communicate and the utter compassion of God in this light, how incredibly daft are we! How terribly we have treated prophets! How stupid it is to ignore a prophet and the message they convey!

Ignoring a prophet becomes even more stupid when the cost of doing so is clearly spelt out for us as in warnings such as these:

Deuteronomy 18:19
Whoever will not heed to my words which he shall speak in my name, I myself shall require it of him.

Ignoring a prophet is not just discarding a man or woman; it is discarding God Himself! It is turning our back on God. It is turning our back on His warnings and grace. This is how serious the situation really is.

God has been persistent in His love and in disclosing His messages. We have been equally persistent in mocking and despising the message and the messengers. Man chooses his path, and when it all goes wrong, even though he was clearly told about the consequences of his actions in advance, what does he do? He blames God. He says, "You have the power; you should sort it out." The trait of humanity is to blame others for the decisions that they take.

The truth is, we are as people generally 'happy' because of our sin to despise God, His word and His messengers. But we do not accept the consequences.

Despising prophets

There are many today that scoff at the idea that prophets still exist. Let us not get 'sucked in' to fruitless and damaging academic arguments that some like to pedal. This is a lie of Satan. What basis do I have for saying this? As part of Peter's sermon he quoted from Joel 2:28,29, saying:

Acts 2:17,18
And in the last days it shall be, God declares, that I will pour out my Spirit upon all flesh, and your sons and your daughters shall prophesy, and your young men shall see visions, and your old men shall dream dreams; yes, and on my menservants and my

maidservants in those days I will pour out my Spirit and they shall prophesy.

Rather than prophets dying out, in the last days God will restore wider communication. Again, if we needed evidence, Paul states these words:

1 Corinthians 12:28
And God has appointed in the church first apostles, second prophets, third teachers, then workers of miracles, then healers, helpers, administrators, speakers in various kinds of tongues.

Prophets are part of the 'fabric' of the church. To suggest that prophets no longer exist is simply untrue and totally unscriptural. Let us never forget that "the household of God [is] built upon the foundation of the apostles and prophets" (Ephesians 2:19). This is why Paul said that "God has appointed in the church first apostles, second prophets" (1 Corinthians 12:28). With Jesus as the cornerstone, "the whole structure is joined together and grows into a holy temple in the Lord; in whom you also are built into it for a dwelling place of God in the Spirit" (Ephesians 2:21,22). The modern-day Church has largely pushed the offices of apostle and prophet into the background – and it does so at its own peril. It is worth re-stating that "the household of God" – the church of true believers – was built upon a foundation; the foundation is "the apostles and prophets".

The incredible fact is there are more references in scripture to the offices of apostle and prophet than to teacher and pastor. Yet how many churches are equipped with, or connected to, all ministries? Oh, that we would wake up and embrace God's word in its entirety; and that we would heed the warning of the fig tree, the warning of our God-inspired prophets! And learn from the errors of our Jewish friends.

All of this leads us to another question that is often raised: is prophecy preaching and teaching?

Are preaching and teaching the same as prophecy?

The French theologian Jehan Cauvin [Jean Calvin], or perhaps more commonly known in England as John Calvin, (1509-1564) was himself confronted with the question 'Is preaching prophecy?'

Calvin considered that 1 Corinthians 14:3, which says, "He who prophesies speaks to men for their upbuilding and encouragement and consolation," indicates that the ability to interpret scripture to meet a current need is prophetic. To put this in another way, he concluded that anyone who interprets God's will is a prophet. This belief is one that has filtered down through time and a view held by many.

Modern-day evangelicals who claim that the gift of prophecy no longer exists find comfort in their Calvinist argument and shift emphasis by saying that the equivalent of prophecy today is preaching and teaching.

When Paul spoke about the use of spiritual gifts he separated teaching from prophecy by saying, "When you come together, each one has a hymn, a lesson, a revelation, a tongue, or an interpretation" (1 Corinthians 14:26). The word 'lesson' used in this scripture is the Greek word *didache* meaning 'teaching' or 'the act of teaching'. The Greek word used for 'revelation' is *apokalypsis;* this means 'to make known hidden secrets, the secrets of heaven'.

The question really centers upon God's revelations. We have already discussed the prophet as God's spokesperson. By way of example I referred earlier to this scripture:

Deuteronomy 18:18
I will raise up for them a prophet like you [Moses] from among their brethren; and I will put my words in his mouth, and he shall speak to them all that I command him.

God has specifically used people He can trust to speak His words. Throughout scripture this has most notably been through those chosen by God and recognized as prophets.

To categorically state that preaching and teaching are equal to prophecy would be misleading and biblically incorrect. There are also many examples of preaching and teaching that are just plain contrary to scripture. This is not to say that someone who preaches and teaches will not have a prophetic word and share this as part of his or her God-inspired discourse. There are many examples of such people who were not or are not prophets per se but bring prophetic words.

Speaking God's message

He did not claim the office of a prophet but during his ministry David Wilkerson (1931-2011) was greatly used by God to prophesy. How we shamefully treated these words and David himself! It is a modern-day travesty that God-fearing Christians should openly be ashamed of. He was not the first to suffer as God's mouthpiece, but – praise God – many doubters and scoffers are now silenced. Do we not realize how brave it is for any man or woman to stand up and speak what God has laid upon their hearts? How instantly we dismiss the prophetic word instead of immediately doing what we should, seeking God!

Yes, of course we must test what we hear. Yes there must be reason and balance applied so that the false prophets are exposed. We must also test those who dare to speak against the prophet and prophecy. By whose authority are they speaking? How well do these people match up to God? What fruits of God do they manifest?

Treating prophets badly

Why do we treat our prophets so badly? The 'bottom line' is that prophets often speak words that we do not want to hear. God may send them into a difficult or volatile situation. They often 'touch a nerve' and expose sin. When convicted, all too often our pride and the fact that we have been 'found out' cause us to become defensive and lash out in some way.

It is important to support what has been said, so by way of illustration let's look at Elijah who faced a backlash from Ahab:

> 1 Kings 18:17,18
> *When Ahab saw Elijah, Ahab said to him, 'Is it you, you troubler of Israel?' And he answered, 'I have not troubled Israel; but you have, and your father's house, because you have forsaken the commandments of the Lord and followed the Baals.'*

In the case of the prophet Zechariah who spoke out against the people for transgressing the commandments of God we read that "they conspired against him, and by command of the king they stoned him" (2 Chronicles 24:21). And again, we read of Jeremiah that "the princes were enraged at Jeremiah, and they beat him and imprisoned him" (Jeremiah 37:15).

Being a prophet can often be a lonely, unappreciated, painful and difficult place to live life. It is important for those who have never been called to give a prophecy to appreciate that delivering a message from God can sometimes be very costly to the messenger. In some cases, as Elijah knew very well, it has cost the prophet their life.

During His sermon on the mount Jesus said:

> Luke 6:22,23
> *Blessed are you when men hate you, and when they exclude you and revile you, and cast out your name as evil, on account of the Son of man! Rejoice in that day, and leap for joy, for behold, your reward is great in heaven; for so their fathers did to the prophets.*

The English evangelist and author Leonard Ravenhill (1907-1994) spoke about the prophet in his writings, entitled 'The Picture of a Prophet', saying:

> *The prophet comes to set up that which is upset. His work is to call into line those who are out of line! He is unpopular because he opposes the popular in morality and spirituality. In a day of faceless politicians and voiceless preachers, there is not a more urgent national need than that we cry to God for a prophet!* [10]

As the church falls into decline with watered-down messages and the infiltration of humanism, we certainly need those who will speak out. Praise God, however, not all is bad news for the prophet. Paul gave us a 'flavour' of how prophecy can positively convict a person who is open to correction when he said:

> 1 Corinthians 14:24,25
> *If all prophesy, and an unbeliever or outsider enters, he is convicted by all, he is called to account by all, the secrets of his heart are disclosed; and so, falling on his face, he will worship God and declare that God is really among you.*

"Dear Lord God, forgive us for treating your chosen servants in such a shameful manner. Many of your faithful servants have paid a terrible price from ridicule and ostracism to hatred and death. We

---

[10] Copyright © 1994 by Leonard Ravenhill, Lindale Texas – *www.ravenhill.org*

owe them not just a debt of gratitude but repentance and our love. Forgive us Lord for despising your prophets and your prophecy. Open our eyes, ears and hearts."

Writing to the Ephesians Paul said:

Ephesians 3:4-6
When you read this you can perceive my insight into the mystery of Christ, which was not made known to the sons of men in other generations as it has now been revealed to his holy apostles and prophets by the Spirit; that is, how the Gentiles are fellow heirs, members of the same body, and partakers of the promise in Christ Jesus through the gospel.

Both Jewish and Gentile people are united in Christ. The scripture verse that heads this chapter reminds us not to "despise prophesying" (1 Thessalonians 5:20).

Being reminded

The English word 'prophesy' is *propheteuo* in the New Testament Greek language and means 'to speak forth by divine inspiration, to foretell future events that relate to the kingdom of God'[11] and so it can include either a declaration of a 'now' message or a future one. The word itself is actually formed as follows: *pro* meaning 'before or beforehand' and *phemi* meaning 'to bring to light, to declare or speak'. It is found on twenty-eight occasions in the New Testament.

A prophet might declare a message that has a short-term outcome, or one that may take many years or even find its fulfillment long after their death. Many prophecies also have a short-term partial fulfillment with a longer-term completeness.

As we discovered earlier, prophecy is specifically included in the list of spiritual gifts found in Ephesians 4:11. Here we also discover the purpose of these gifts bestowed upon people along with a clear sign of how long the role will remain a necessary office. Take a look at these words:

---

[11] Please refer to the bibliography for reference sources.

Ephesians 4:12-14

To equip the saints for the work of ministry, for building up the body of Christ [the purpose], until we all attain to the unity of the faith and of the knowledge of the Son of God, to mature manhood, to the measure of the stature of the fullness of Christ; so that we may no longer be children, tossed to and fro and carried about with every wind of doctrine, by the cunning of men, by their craftiness in deceitful wiles.

The prophet will be in ministry "until we all attain to the unity of the faith and of the knowledge of the Son of God, to mature manhood, to the measure of the stature of the fullness of Christ". Anyone who says that the ministry of the prophet is dead or no longer needed needs to re-visit this scripture. It says "until we all" – that means everyone, every believer. I would not wish to criticize others, but I can confess that I have not reached this "measure of the stature of the fullness of Christ!" I am part of the "all" and so the prophet must still be in ministry.

This all sounds reasonably straightforward and logical, but let's also remember that Jesus issued a stern warning. The warning was, "Beware of false prophets, who come to you in sheep's clothing but inwardly are ravenous wolves" (Matthew 7:15). What we learn from this and our investigation so far is that there are both genuine and false prophets.

Why am I reminding us of this fact? Because this is as true today as it has always been. In fact, the number of false prophets and prophecies has increased over the last few decades. When we couple this with our opening scripture from 1 Thessalonians, which tells us, "Do not despise prophesying," (1 Thessalonians 5:20) a potential dilemma confronts us, especially when we also reconsider the words I quoted from earlier: "Whoever will not give heed to my words which he [the prophet] shall speak in my name, I myself will require it of him" (Deuteronomy 18:19). This leads us to another question: how do we know what to accept and what to flee from?

Knowing the true prophet

In the scriptures that I have quoted, namely Matthew 7:15ff and 1 Thessalonians 5:20ff, help is usefully suggested that will keep our focus clear about the identity of true and false prophets.

Matthew 7:16-20
You will know them by their fruits. Are grapes gathered from thorns, or figs from thistles? So, every sound tree bears good fruit, but the bad tree bears evil fruit. A sound tree cannot bear evil fruit, nor can a bad tree bear good fruit. Every tree that does not bear good fruit is cut down and thrown into the fire. Thus you will know them by their fruit.

We will "know them by their fruit". What Jesus is expressing is that what a prophet says will at some point show itself as truth or a lie.

This same concern about true and false prophecy was previously raised and answered by God in His statement found in the Old Testament book of Deuteronomy. In this scripture we find a prediction about the coming Messiah, Jesus. But a stern warning to would-be prophets is forcefully issued along with advice on how to test those prophets who are false. God says:

Deuteronomy 18:20-22
The prophet who presumes to speak a word in my name which I have not commanded him to speak, or who speaks in the name of other gods, that same prophet shall die. And if you say in your heart, 'How may we know the word which the Lord has not spoken?' – when a prophet speaks in the name of the Lord, if the word does not come to pass or come true, that is a word which the Lord has not spoken; the prophet has spoken it presumptuously; you need not be afraid of him.

These are very powerful words. If anyone is going to give a word of prophecy it must come from God. We will know if it is from God because it will come to pass.

The warning is that a false prophet 'shall die'. The Hebrew word used here is *muwth* meaning 'to die prematurely'. It is a shortening of the prophet's physical life, but also it is figurative – a social death by neglect. In other words we are to turn away from and discard this prophecy. Having tested the prophecy and found it to be false we have no need to fear what the 'prophet' might say. God will deal with them.

What we are uncovering is that prophecy is a means that God uses to communicate to people and that it is very important to the Christian believer. To ignore a genuine prophet and prophecy is unwise to the extreme. We should certainly not be surprised that

Satan knows this, and so he does everything that he can to subtly mimic God's word and deceive all who will listen to those who want to pull us away from the truth.

Satan knows that his time is short. The intensity of the battle for our minds and to steer us off course is increasing in these last days. He is using every opportunity and device to drag as many people down with him as possible. Any way that he can use to make the Church ineffective will be, and is stealthily being, used. Some of these tactics are so subtle that we embrace them, such as doing good, helping the needy – but crucially not actually preaching the gospel. Good works do not worry Satan. The gospel message on the other hand scares him.

Being ignorant of what the Bible has to say through lack of time in the word of God, having poor day-by-day relationship with God and closing our ears to what God is saying leave us vulnerable and easy pickings for Satan's deceptions. This begs the question then, how can we recognize truth from falsehood?

Some examples of how to identify a true prophet are as follows:

1 Corinthians 14:3,4
He who prophesies speaks to men for their up building, and encouragement and consolation. He who speaks in a tongue edifies himself, but he who prophesies edifies the church.

2 Peter 1:21
No prophecy ever came by the impulse of man, but men moved by the Holy Spirit spoke from God.

1 John 4:1-3
Do not believe every spirit, but test the spirits to see whether they are of God; for many false prophets have gone out into the world. By this you know the Spirit of God: every spirit, which confesses that Jesus Christ has come in the flesh is of God, and every spirit, which does not confess Jesus is not of God. This is the spirit of antichrist, of which you heard that it was coming, and now it is in the world already.

Deuteronomy 13:1-3
If a prophet arises among you, or a dreamer of dreams and gives you a sign or a wonder, and the sign or wonder which he tells you comes to pass, and if he says, 'Let us go after other gods', which you have not known, 'and let us serve them', you shall not listen to the words of that prophet or to that dreamer of dreams;

for the Lord your God is testing you, to know whether you love the Lord your God with all your heart and with all your soul.

Jeremiah 23:16,17
Do not listen to the words of the prophets who prophesy to you, filling you with vain hopes; they speak visions of their own minds, not from the mouth of the Lord. They say continually to those who despise the word of the Lord, 'It shall be well with you'; and to every one who stubbornly follow his own heart, they say, 'No evil shall come upon you'.

Galatians 1:8
Even if we, or an angel from heaven, should preach to you a gospel contrary to that which we preached to you, let him be accursed.

Having made these points it should be said that it may not always be that easy to distinguish a false prophet from a true one. The best lies and deceptions are those that mimic truth and are 99% true. False prophets may do signs and miracles. Some things they say may come to pass. They may even seem to cast out demons or speak in a tongue. Jesus recognized this fact and said:

Matthew 7:22,23
On that day many will say to me, 'Lord, Lord, did we not prophesy in your name, and cast out demons in your name, and do many mighty works in your name?' And then will I declare to them, 'I never knew you; depart from me, you evildoers.'

The really interesting and significant part of this statement is "I never knew you; depart from me, you evildoers" (verse 23). The King James Version puts it this way: "I never knew you; depart from me, you who practice lawlessness." The Greek translation for 'practice lawlessness' is *ergazomai anomia*.

- *Ergazomai* means 'to work, labour, trade or do business'.
- *Anomia* means 'to be ignorant of or to violate or have contempt for the law'.

Jesus recognized those who outwardly appear to do good things but their inner intent is evil. Evil will in some way manifest itself.

A true prophet will always speak in absolute accordance with scripture. They will always speak against sin, and they will stay true to the faith, to God, Jesus and the Holy Spirit. The Holy Spirit will be clearly evident in them though we must also appreciate that a person, particularly a fledgling prophet, might be 'imperfect'. What I mean here is that their thoughts and enthusiasm may mingle with those of God and so not come to pass. These will not however be contrary to scripture.

There is another aspect of prophecy that we seldom hear explained. It is an aspect that we must make sure we are aware of; otherwise we will misunderstand the purpose and occasional result of a prophetic word. I am here referring to that fact that *not all prophecy has to come to fruition*. But what does this mean?

A prophetic word does not have to be fulfilled

It is important that we grasp the fact that some prophecies are accurately delivered but not necessarily fulfilled. This does not mean that the prophet was wrong or misguided. The point that I am making is that some prophecies *do not need* fulfillment.

Let me explain. If we turn to the Old Testament book of Jonah we come across the story of a reluctant but nonetheless eventually obedient prophet who had reached this point having learned a salutary lesson.

We read that Jonah received a prophetic word for the inhabitants of Nineveh. God said to Jonah, "Go to Nineveh, that great city, and proclaim to it the message that I tell you" (Jonah 3:2). Jonah went on a three-day journey to the city. When he arrived Jonah proclaimed the prophetic word, "Yet forty days, and Nineveh shall be overthrown!" (Jonah 3:4). What happened next was one of the fastest turnarounds ever seen among an entire group of city dwellers. The people took heed of the prophecy. They immediately acknowledged God's word and they repented. The entire city humbled themselves before God.

As we follow the story and see the people's penitence and turning from their evil ways a remarkable thing happens. We read these words:

Jonah 3:10
God saw what they did, how they turned from their evil way, God repented of the evil which he had said he would do to them; and he did not do it.

Jonah was a little upset and said that he had told God they would react that way. But the point is both Jonah and the people of Nineveh acted obediently and God rewarded them.

Some words of prophecy carry with them 'if' messages – or to put this in another, more correct way they are *conditional* prophecies. For example, Moses said to the people:

> Deuteronomy 28:1
> *If you obey the Lord your God, being careful to do all his commandments which I command you this day, the Lord your God will set you high above all the nations of the earth.*

This statement is then followed by several further benefits that come with the obedience. We also read however:

> Deuteronomy 28:15
> *But if you will not obey the voice of the Lord your God or be careful to do all his commandments and his statutes which I command you this day, then all these curses shall come upon you and overtake you.*

What we see shown in these examples of conditional prophecies are God's warnings and the open door of grace and mercy. Jeremiah explains this for us in these prophetic words:

> Jeremiah 18:7,8
> *If at any time I declare concerning a nation or kingdom, that I will pluck up and break down and destroy it, and if that nation, concerning which I have spoken, turns from its evil, I will repent of the evil that I intended to do to it.*

But let us not stop here. As we read further the converse is also true. If good is declared but evil comes in then the good that was originally declared will instead be taken away.

A prophetic word does not have to be sequential

A study of scripture and prophecy demonstrates that the prophetic word does not necessarily run consecutively or sequentially. It also shows that 'nuggets' of prophecy are actually scattered throughout the Bible. There are also occasions where a time-lapse takes place between one aspect of the prophecy and another. Sometimes there is a partial fulfillment or 'taster' that precedes the main prophecy. Some prophecies even have several stages and are fulfilled in multiple ways.

By way of illustration let's take a look at two examples from the Old Testament:

Isaiah 9:6,7

For to us a child is born, to us a son is given; and the government will be upon his shoulder, and his name will be called, 'Wonderful Counselor, Mighty God, Everlasting Father, Prince of Peace.' Of the increase of his government and of peace there will be no end, upon the throne of David, and over his kingdom, to establish it, and to uphold it with justice and with righteousness from this time forth and for evermore. The zeal of the Lord will do this.

In the short term some Bible scholars see this as a prophecy about the birth of Hezekiah. Whether this is right or not, what is clear is the fact that this prophecy foretells the birth and life of Jesus. But it also 'jumps' time to include the eventual place of Jesus the Messiah.

Zechariah 9:9,10

Rejoice greatly, O daughter of Zion! Shout aloud, O daughter of Jerusalem! Lo, your king comes to you; triumphant and victorious is he, humble and riding on an ass, on a colt the foal of an ass. I will cut off the chariot from Ephraim and the war horse from Jerusalem; and the battle bow shall be cut off, and he shall command peace to the nations; his dominion shall be from sea to sea, and from the River to the ends of the earth.

In this prophecy we have a 'filling in' or a little more detail of part of Isaiah's prophecy. Yet again though, we see a time jump from the arrival of Jesus into Jerusalem on the back of a colt to the close of the age.

An amazing fact is that nearly one third of the entire Bible is actually prophecy. Another amazing fact is that apart from the very last day prophecies (those still to come because we have not reached their timing yet) and those where repentance has intervened to invoke God's grace and mercy, every prophetic statement made in scripture has actually been fulfilled.

After His resurrection Jesus appeared to His disciples and said:

Luke 24:44
*These are my words that I spoke to you, while I was with you,
that everything written about me in the Law of Moses and the
prophets and the psalms must be fulfilled.*

The Old Testament has over forty prophecies telling of the
coming of Jesus. Every one of these was perfectly fulfilled. Isaiah
records these words:

Isaiah 46:9,10
*Remember the former things of old; for I am God, and there is
none like me, declaring the end from the beginning and from
ancient times things not yet done, saying, 'My counsel shall
stand, and I will accomplish all my purpose'.*

God has declared His purposes and He will fulfil them.

Declarations of God

In order to revitalize and stir us let's take a look at just a couple
of the declarations of God. One of the features of these, as mentioned
already, is that fulfillment of prophecies can either experience time
delays over hundreds of years or find fulfillment in relatively short
time spans. Those who want to discredit God's prophecies often
overlook this point. They also tend to overlook that even if a
prophecy has a short time span in its fulfillment it is still a prophecy
that has actually been fulfilled!

To illustrate this point let's take a look at Isaiah's prophetic
words about the sign of a virgin birth which would bring defeat to
the people's enemies. Isaiah said to frightened King Ahaz:

Isaiah 7:14
*The Lord himself will give you a sign. Behold, a young woman
shall conceive and bear a son, and shall call his name Immanuel
[meaning 'God is with us'].*

The King James Version says, "Behold, the virgin shall conceive
and bear a son." This translation is actually closer to the original
Hebrew, which says, *"hinneh almah hareh yalad ben."* Roughly
translated this means, "Behold, see or look, a virgin young woman,
pregnant with child, a little girl with a son."

As we read on into the New Testament we discover details of the
fulfillment of this prophecy. This sign is clearly established within a

comparatively short time span. Having been encouraged we are then introduced to another linking prophecy statement that takes the first into new territory; Isaiah declares:

Isaiah 9:6
For to us a child is born, to us a child is given; and the government will be upon his shoulder, and his name will be called, 'Wonderful, Counsellor, Mighty God, Everlasting Father, Prince of Peace.'

The birth of the Son of God is accurately predicted. This wonderful gift of God leads all Christian believers to become part of the prophetic testimony of Christ.

Before leaving these thoughts let us remind ourselves that we must always keep in mind that the Bible speaks in the language and experience of its time. It does not speak about modern warfare equipment. It does not speak about the countries that now exist but were not present during that time. Not only must we test scripture but we must also view it in the light and understanding of the time in which it was actually written and apply this knowledge to our modern geography. Bible scholars often forget to make the transitions, and confusion can ensue. Dear friend, let's be careful not to dismiss God's prophecies just because Bible scholars make academic statements that seem to suggest a different outcome. God's word is truth, and it can be wholly relied upon. Even though we may not understand what Jesus had to say, it was truth.

The spirit of prophecy

In the words of Revelation 19:10 quoted earlier we read that "the testimony of Jesus is the spirit of prophecy". But what does this mean, and what relevance does it have for those who believe in the Lord Jesus Christ?

When writing to the Corinthian church Paul made this bold statement:

1 Corinthians 14:1
Make love your aim, and earnestly desire the spiritual gifts, especially that you may prophesy.

Every Christian believer should passionately want to prophesy! Why? Paul goes on to say:

1 Corinthians 14:3
He who prophesies speaks to men for their upbuilding and encouragement and consolation.

In love, through prophecy the Christian believer builds, encourages and consoles.

"Well," some of you may say, "I am not a prophet. I am not used by God to prophesy." Dear friend, this is not entirely true. In these few verses Paul links prophecy with the words that we read from Revelation. The heart, the spirit of prophecy, is the testimony of Jesus. Every believer, every person who has found the path of salvation through Christ possesses this anointed prophecy. We are all called to preach the gospel to the nations, and so the spirit of prophecy, the testimony of our salvation, is that means by which we daily share with those whom God brings across our path so that we can build, encourage, console, set free and regenerate them.

As we testify what Jesus has done for us – the blood of Calvary, the transformation of our lives – we speak of our salvation. It is a salvation that we will receive in its fullness when we die and go to heaven. We are in this sense prophesying our heavenly homeland. This is eternity in the kingdom of God available to all who receive Jesus as Lord and saviour now.

I could not hope to round this thought off in any better way than with the words of Smith Wigglesworth who, talking about why testimonial prophecy is important, said:[12]

Because prophecy by the power of the Spirit is the only power that saves humanity. We are told in the word of God that the Gospel that is presented through prophecy has power to bring immortality and light.

Wigglesworth was referring here to the words written by Paul to Timothy saying that there should be no shame felt over testifying the gospel of Jesus who "abolished death and brought life and immortality to light through the gospel" (2 Timothy 1:10). The immortality here is *spiritual* immortality. It is speaking of, and prophesying, life in the kingdom of God. The 'light' is the light of

---

[12] Taken from *Smith Wigglesworth Devotional* by Smith Wigglesworth. Copyright © (1999) by Whitaker House. Used by permission of Whitaker House. *www.whitakerhouse.com*

God's word and the gospel message that reveals the sinful condition of man and the need for salvation.

Closing thoughts

Many will argue about the proven authenticity of prophecy. They will also say that New Testament writers twisted the facts of their day to fit Old Testament writings. The 'bottom line', as far as I am concerned, is that the Bible is God's word. It is truth and it is reliable. But our faith is not vague – "Faith comes from what is heard" (Romans 10:17). What is heard must also be preached or taught. A faith that is not based upon knowledge will always falter.

Let's take a look at some examples of fulfilled prophecies for which it would be impossible for the outcome to have been 'tampered'.

Psalm 22:15-18

My tongue cleaves to my jaws; thou dost lay me in the dust of death. Yea, dogs are round about me; a company of evildoers encircle me; they have pierced my hands and feet – I can count all my bones – they stare and gloat over me; they divide my garments among them, and for my raiment they cast lots.

When we read the account of the crucifixion in John 19:28-37 we discover that this prophecy was clearly fulfilled. John is candid in his summation of these events:

These things took place that the scripture might be fulfilled, 'Not a bone of him shall be broken'. And again another scripture says, 'They shall look on him whom they have pierced.

Also, Matthew 27:35 explains the amazing fulfillment of the prophecy that lots would be cast for His raiment:

They divided his garments among them by casting lots.

The prophecies that Jesus would be nailed to the cross, that none of His bones would be broken and that lots would be cast for His clothing could not have been accurately predicted so far in advance unless supernaturally inspired.

Isaiah 53:9
And they made his grave with the wicked and with a rich man in his death, although he had done no violence, and there was no deceit in his mouth.

Matthew 27: 38
Then two robbers were crucified with him, one on the right and one on the left.

In Matthew 27:57-60, Joseph of Arimathea, a rich man, buried Jesus in a tomb that had been ready for his own body – not that of a stranger.

Bible scholars have calculated that there are well over twelve hundred prophecies in the Old Testament and nearly five hundred and eighty New Testament prophecies. As I stated earlier, taking into account God's grace and mercy there has been a one hundred percent success rate in fulfillment of prophecies so far. Given this rate of accuracy it is not unreasonable to accept that all Bible prophecy will eventually be fulfilled. The point being made here is that the godly authenticity of scripture is clear through the incredible accuracy of prophecy fulfillment.

We now live in an age where perhaps like no other we need to "walk by the Spirit" (Galatians 5:16). This has always been important, but now is a time to cry out to God for the Holy Spirit, for wisdom and discernment. The apostle Paul prayed for the church in Philippi and he said:

Philippians 1:9-11
It is my prayer that your love may abound more and more, with knowledge and all discernment, so that you may approve what is excellent, and may be pure and blameless for the day of Christ, filled with the fruits of righteousness which come through Jesus Christ, to the glory and praise of God.

I do not know about you but this prayer is one that I plead God will reawaken in my life and in the life of the church. I want the knowledge and discernment necessary to separate what is good from evil. I want my life approved and counted as blameless. I want my life filled with the fruits of righteousness that come through Jesus Christ my Lord and saviour. I want to glorify and praise God.

We live in an era in which our prayer really needs to mirror that of Solomon who said, "Give to your servant an understanding heart [the Revised Standard Version says 'mind'] ... that I may discern between good and evil" (1 Kings 3:9, KJV).

We must keep a balance – not falling into the trap that Abraham fell into by trying to hasten God's timing through his own plans, and yet staying alert by going along with the flow of God's timing and purposes. Prophecy should cause us to keep looking at God and in these last days to eagerly expect the return of Jesus by being equally alert and fully prepared.

> 1 Corinthians 14:1-5
>
> *Make love your aim, and earnestly desire the spiritual gifts, especially that you may prophesy. For one who speaks in a tongue speaks not to men but to God; for no one understands him, but he utters mysteries in the Spirit. On the other hand, he who prophesies speaks to men for their upbuilding and encouragement and consolation. He who speaks in a tongue edifies himself, but he who prophesies edifies the church. Now I want you all to speak in tongues, but even more to prophesy. He who prophesies is greater than he who speaks in tongues, unless some one interprets, so that the church may be edified.*

Chapter Two

Knowing the Signs

Ezekiel 37:21,22

Thus says the Lord God: Behold, I will take the people of Israel from the nations among which they have gone, and will gather them from all sides, and bring them to their own land; and I will make them one nation in the land, upon the mountains of Israel; and one king shall be king over them all; and they shall be no longer two nations, and no longer divided into two kingdoms'

Seed Thought

Revelation 1:7 (NIV)

Look, he is coming with the clouds, and 'every eye will see him, even those who pierced him'; and all peoples on earth 'will mourn because of him'. So shall it be! Amen.

Introduction

Jesus said, "When I go and prepare a place for you, I will come again and will take you to myself, that where I am you may be also" (John 14:3). In these few words Jesus made a precious promise that He would one day return and take His faithful followers so that they will be permanently with him. But to the question when He would return Jesus said, "Of that day or that hour no one knows, not even the angels in heaven, nor the Son, but only the Father" (Mark 13:32). It is quite clear from this scripture verse that although Jesus has promised to return no one knows and no one *can* know when His revisit will take place. Although this specific information has and will be kept concealed it is also very clear that God wants us fully aware of the signs that herald the second coming.

I concluded the first chapter by making the point that watching the signs is neither about us trying to pre-empt God's plans or sitting back with our spiritual feet in the air and doing nothing. It is about trusting Him and keeping our gaze upon Him. If God wants us aware of the signs then it is logical to accept that He must want us fully prepared and ready.

People from all walks of life, not necessarily believers, are saying that we are living in extraordinary times. We are constantly battered by global economic problems, weather changes, disasters and destructions. Those watching the sun and planets talk about impending problems, and some even say that we are nearing the end of time, the age and even of life. Terrorism is a 'new' war, and threats are often and increasingly being made against Israel. Society is breaking down, and atrocities (as well as what can only be described as 'rip offs') are abounding as people and companies alike are seeking to profit at the cost of the vulnerable. Society is breaking down.

What most people do not realize is that all of this in one way or another is foretold in scripture. The return of Jesus is in the signs.

What are the signs?

Talking about His second coming, Jesus made some very clear statements when He said:

> Luke 21:25-28
> *And there will be signs in sun and moon and stars, and upon the earth distress of nations in perplexity at the roaring of the sea and the waves, men fainting with fear and with foreboding of what is coming on the world; for the powers of the heavens will be shaken. And then they will see the Son of man coming in a cloud with power and great glory. Now when these things begin to take place, look up and raise your hands, because your redemption is drawing near.*

As we see these things unfolding Jesus said, "Look up and raise your hands."

The Greek word for 'signs' used in this scripture text is *semeion*, which in our modern English language would probably be written as 'an unusual occurrence, a distinguishing sign' or we might even say 'a sign of the times'. The same word in Hebrew is *owt* meaning 'a supernatural mark, a proof or a warning'. Examples of these would be the blood on the doorposts described in Exodus 12:7 signifying protection, the rainbow of Genesis 9:13 given as a promise, and the star that the wise men observed in Matthew 2:2 proclaiming that Jesus had arrived.

The signs that God gives are specifically designed for such purpose as covenants, protection, proclamations and warnings.

Peter wrote about the second coming of Jesus, saying:

2 Peter 3:2-4
Remember the predictions of the holy prophets and the commandment of the Lord and Saviour through your apostles. First of all you must understand this, that scoffers will come in the last days with scoffing, following their own passions and saying, 'Where is the promise of his coming? For ever since the fathers fell asleep, all things have continued as they were from the beginning of creation.'

It is a shocking fact that some of these scoffers are found in our churches. It is also a shocking fact that Christian argues against Christian. Appetite for revival is painfully low, and even lower is an appetite to pay the price for a supernatural lifestyle.

In Paul's first letter to Timothy we find these words:

1 Timothy 4:1,2
The Spirit expressly says that in the later times some will depart from the faith by giving heed to deceitful spirits and doctrines, through the pretensions of liars whose consciences are seared.

Deceitful spirits and doctrines bombard us today. Jesus even warned that these might deceive the elect (Matthew 24:24). We have a great need to pay close attention and listen to the Holy Spirit. When we sense something is not right in our spirit it is a sure sign to apply great caution and not get swept away with the 'crowd'.

I cannot think of a time in my personal experience when it has been so noticeable that all Christian denominations – charismatic and evangelical alike – have mostly lost their way to one degree or another. The sad thing is many within these environs do not even know or recognize it. These are all signs, among many, many more, that show the closing of the age.

We know that one of the signs of the end will be famine. This is often misunderstood to refer solely to food shortages. Amos tells us that there is more to the meaning of famine, and this sits right beneath our noses, many being totally oblivious to it. In order to make sure that we do not stay oblivious let's take a look at what Amos said:

Amos 8:11
'Behold, the days are coming' says the Lord God, 'when I will send a famine on the land; not a famine of bread, nor a thirst for water, but of hearing the words of the Lord'.

Try as some might to find the word being spoken and preached in its undiluted, pure and anointed form, it will rarely be found.

It is a bitter pill for many to swallow but if you wanted to find a sign that things are not right and something terrible is imminently being unleashed, it faces us week by week in our churches. A cocktail of diluted messages, humanism and little or no evidence of supernatural living find many Christians week-by-week content with what is actually second best.

I hear it said so often: "It is hard to find a good church." Or perhaps even more worrying is Christians proclaiming that they get a good word when in fact it is lackluster and lacking in anointing. Let's be honest before God – is what we hear and experience anointed and supernaturally supported? Our aim should daily be to "seek first his kingdom and his righteousness" (Matthew 6:33). Where has our ache for the supernatural and revival gone? Where is the proof of our faith?

Our Jewish friends were well aware of the prophecies and signs of the coming Messiah, Jesus. But at the time of Jesus many did not (and some still do not) recognize the signs, pay attention to them and act. In this sense they missed out. They know the Old Testament scriptures in a way that puts many to shame, but this knowledge has not (until comparatively recent times) been so distinctive when it comes to the New Testament. Of all people, what was facing them was by and large missed. This statement is perhaps better illustrated in these words:

Matthew 12:23
Can this be the Son of David?

The people had just witnessed the healing of a demoniac, but the Pharisees stepped in to deflect the truth. What we can learn from this is that knowing about the signs and recognizing them are two very different things.

Admittedly the second coming of Jesus will be dramatic, and of course it will be one of the last acts; but are we watching the signs? Can we recognize them? Are we looking for the kingdom? Will we be ready, or will we miss out like the foolish maidens? Of course, those who believe they are safe may have viewed many of these questions as superfluous. But are they?

Unhelpful controversy exists about the question of whether salvation can actually be lost. This controversy causes some Christians to become complacent and others to act as if whatever they do, they are okay. Scripture does not place such a bold and confident view for us to live by in this way.

In the first letter of Peter we are given warning that our "adversary the devil prowls around like a roaring lion, seeking someone to devour" (1 Peter 5:8). We must remain on our guard at all times and seek to live in humble holiness before God. Let's consider a few scriptures that may help us to deal with this question more soberly:

Hebrews 3:14
For we share in Christ, if only we hold our first confidence firm to the end.

Matthew 7:22,23
Lord, Lord, did we not prophesy in your name, and cast out demons in your name, and do many mighty works in your name? And then will I declare to them, 'I never knew you; depart from me, you evildoers.'

Romans 11:22,23
Note then the kindness and the severity of God: severity toward those who have fallen, but God's kindness to you, provided you continue in his kindness; otherwise you too will be cut off. And even the others, if they do not persist in their unbelief, will be grafted in, for God has the power to graft them in again.

1 Corinthians 9:27
I pommel my body and subdue it, lest after preaching to others I myself should be disqualified.

Romans 8:13
If you live according to the flesh you will die, but if by the Spirit you put to death the deeds of the body you will live.

These scripture verses, however we may wish to interpret them, do at least point us toward erring on the side of safety. Why do we think that Jesus himself gave so many warnings about being ready? Why did He liken it to the days of Noah? We need to read and study the Bible under the supernatural guidance of the Holy Spirit, not according to man's interpretations.

Let's be ready. Let's be found working tirelessly to bringing as much of the harvest to the kingdom as we can. Let us be found as worthy servants and good stewards who have kept the faith. If nothing else is eventually achieved from this chapter I hope that the message of preparation, alertness and readiness will not only be taken to heart but also acted upon.

These opening thoughts lead us to ask, what are the signs that we need to take careful note of?

Midnight on the 14th / 15th May 1948 should resonate in every Gentile Christian believer's heart and mind. This date should strike godly fear into the hearts of those who do not truly believe God's promises or those who fail to take heed of His word in scripture and the many prophecies that have demonstrably been fulfilled. If this date does not strike a chord or bring holy fear upon us then something is terribly wrong. Something is missing in our relationship with God. This message applies to everyone whether Christian believer or non-believer. It also signals the last opportunity for the Jewish people to find their way back to Adonai.[13]

How profound! You may of course be questioning and wondering why such an odd (and certainly bold and uncompromising) statement has been made. Of course a statement like this must also be answered, explained and supported. You are therefore invited to join

---

[13] Also spelt *A-donaj*, the name used by the Jewish people for God in prayer. Outside of prayer they say *Ha Shem* (the Name) and *Yeshua* (Jesus). As an aside, though an important one for the Christian Church to understand, Jewish people do not call God *Jehovah*. The names or titles of God are a complex subject, and there is some debate about how the word Jehovah was first used, possibly a transliteration corruption of *Yhyh* (occasionally written as *Yhvh*). These four letters are sometimes referred to as the Tetragrammaton, a word literally meaning 'four letters'.

with me on a journey of discovery upon which I believe God will open our hearts to deeper truths about Himself and His purposes.

In order to answer this question we need first to come humbly before God and prayerfully retrace some events in recent modern-day history and compare these with Bible prophecy. This process needs to be undertaken free of political views, preconceptions and bias. It is not about politics. Rather it is about approaching God's word with an open heart and a genuine desire to have our spiritual eyes and ears opened. Otherwise the 'mysteries' of God will remain just that – mysteries – and we will inevitably not be ready for what is yet to come.

Background information

This section is a brief outline to set the scene and introduce the scenario that will lead us into end time prophecies. Written around the period when the Jewish nation was first formed, the Old Testament books of Leviticus and Deuteronomy give warnings about the consequences of rebelling against God and His word. The clearly stated repercussions of disobedience were spelt out, and the later Roman slaughter of the Jewish people that we will look at shortly was foretold in these words:

> Deuteronomy 28:49-52
> *The Lord will bring a nation against you from afar, from the end of the earth, as swift as the eagle flies, a nation whose language you do not understand, a nation of stern countenance, who shall not regard the person of the old or show favour to the young, and shall eat the offspring of your cattle and the fruit of your ground, until you are destroyed; who also shall not leave you grain, wine, or oil, the increase of your cattle or the young of your flock, until they have caused you to perish. They shall besiege you in all your towns, until your high and fortified walls, in which you trusted, come down throughout all your land; and they shall besiege you in all your towns throughout all your land, which the Lord your God has given you.*

Of course we now know that although fair warning was given the Israelites continued to disobey and murmur against God. The rest of the Old Testament shows how God tried to keep His people in check and how they persisted in their disobedience, which eventually led to and caused their own downfall.

Through the 'spectacles' of hindsight and history we have the benefit of looking at the rise and fall of the Jewish nation and seeing the lengths to which God was willing to go to stop His chosen people from self-destruction. What, however, has humanity really learned?

There is a saying that says, "Learn from your mistakes or learn from the mistakes of others." Of course, one can only learn from a mistake if one first recognizes a mistake has been made. Having done this, the next stage is to personally admit to it. In reality, what often happens is that we blame others; or we blame situations and circumstances and deny our part, our responsability.

Generally we do not like to admit or accept that we are wrong (or even may prove to be wrong). Our self-defence mechanism kicks in because we are (or may feel) threatened. As soon as we find ourselves in this scenario any chance of learning from the situation disappears and we 'dig our heels in'. This is a dangerous place to get into because it leaves us wide open to attack from Satan and the subtleties of deception. It is partly for this reason that humility before God is so important.

Learning from mistakes can only be achieved when we change our outlook, forgive others and ourselves and take personal responsibility. It comes when we turn away from what we were doing or not doing and keep looking for anything that may help us to stay focused on God. The truth is mistakes are opportunities to change, find a different way and improve. This way of thinking is an important and vital mind shift for many. Added to this is the mind shift from what I will call 'defeated acceptance' – the mistake of accepting second best rather than going in unquenchable pursuit of God and the best that He can offer.

The Jewish people did not learn from their mistakes. But we, as Gentiles, have a perfect opportunity to learn from the mistakes that they have made – to see how God is truth and love and look for the warning signs. We not only have this golden opportunity to learn but also to take the gospel message back to God's chosen people in love.

We have much to thank our Jewish friends for. They have jealously and meticulously guarded the writings of God through terrible adversity and hardship. We owe them much more than we perhaps realize.

Moving the story on, we know that Jesus died just before the Passover feast in approximately 33AD (give or take a few years). Before his death Jesus told a series of parables including the parable of the fig tree (Matthew 24:32-35) and the early stages or what we might refer to today as the 'Braxton Hicks' birth pangs of the end days: the faithful and unfaithful servants (Matthew 24:45-51) and the ten virgins (Matthew 25:1-13). The following is a summary of what Jesus said about the signs of the last days in chapters twenty-four and twenty-five of the Gospel of Matthew:

- Many will come claiming that they are Christ.
- There will be wars and rumours of wars.
- Nations and kingdoms will rise up against one another.
- There will be famines and earthquakes.
- We will be mercilessly delivered up to tribulation – hated and put to death.
- Many will fall away.
- Many false prophets will arise.
- Men's hearts will grow cold.
- The gospel will first be preached to all nations.

Having declared these things Jesus then turned His attention to the prophecy of Daniel and said to His disciples:

Matthew 24:15,16
When you see the desolating sacrilege spoken by the prophet Daniel, standing in the holy place (let the reader understand), then let those who are in Judea flee to the mountains.

The fact that Jesus highlighted Daniel's prophecy means that there is something specific that He wants us to check out. It is for this reason that we will take a closer look at this later.

Jesus then concluded with the following statement (that some have misrepresented):

Matthew 24:34
Truly, I say to you, this generation will not pass away till all these things take place.

The statement "This generation will not pass away till all these things take place" has put many Christians, theologians and Bible scholars into a 'spin' and confusion. Before I go further on this point, I am not suggesting here that a Christian, theologian and Bible scholar are the same or that they are necessarily all true believers. Suffice to say at this point that understanding God's word is relational and Spirit-led. Natural intelligence and background are not a measure of a person's ability to grasp and understand the Bible. Paul highlights this thought for us in these words:

> **1 Corinthians 1:18**
> *The word of the cross is folly to those who are perishing, but to us who are being saved it is the power of God.*

There are many examples of people who have been mightily used by God but have humble backgrounds, no theological training or even have also been regarded as of 'lower' intelligence: William Branham (1909-1965), a rancher and boxer; John Bunyan (1628-1688), a tinker; William Carey (1761-1834), a cobbler; Dwight Moody (1837-1899), a shoe salesman; and Smith Wigglesworth (1859-1947), a plumber. These are just some examples of people from humble backgrounds, for some of whom academia was not a strong point and the world would have rejected. But God used these people mightily.

In scripture we read:

> **Acts 4:13**
> *When they saw the boldness of Peter and John, and perceived that they were uneducated, common men, they wondered; and they recognized that they had been with Jesus.*

The fact that Peter and John had not been formally educated meant that their eloquence before the Sanhedrin had a greater impact. Paul put it this way:

> **1 Corinthians 1:26,27**
> *Consider your call, brethren; not many of you were wise according to worldly standards, not many were powerful, not many were of noble birth; but God chose what is foolish in the world to shame the wise, God chose what is weak in the world to shame the strong.*

And again Paul goes on to offer an insight about these things and explains why it is possible for an 'ordinary' person to dumfound a scholar:

1 Corinthians 2:14
The unspiritual man does not receive the gifts of the Spirit of God, for they are folly to him, and he is not able to understand them because they are spiritually discerned.

Returning to the earlier point, part of the problem is that many who question statements like, "This generation will not pass away till all these things take place," simply do not accept scripture as the true word of God and that it is infallible and the truth. They are looking for errors and mistakes or something to criticize and prove themselves right. There is a very big difference between searching the scriptures with a pure heart and wanting to know more about God and digging to prove a personal point and discredit God. Another aspect to the problem finds its roots in misunderstanding, lack of knowledge and understanding because a lack of relationship with God and time spent with Him in prayer and reading the scriptures exists.

An assumption is often made that Jesus is talking in Matthew 24 purely about the close of the age but this was actually only part of the picture. Why do I say this?

Let's take a closer look at why Jesus has exercised the minds of many Bible scholars by saying, "*This generation* will not pass away till all these things take place." In our-modern day English language we would interpret "this generation" to mean 'all those living at the time that the statement occurred' or 'all those of a particular or specified birth period'. It would be a foreseeable time span within the lifespan of the group.

When we look at the Greek words for 'this generation' used in the context of this verse we discover that they are *houtos genea* meaning 'this or these successive members of a genealogy and the multitude of civilization that are living at any one time'. To put this in another way *genea* refers to both the present generation and future generations.

The other part of what Jesus said was "till all these things take place". What Jesus was clearly saying is that what He had predicted would take place within their generation – but that it would also be a sign for a generation yet to come. Jesus was in actual fact making prophetic statements that had both short-term and longer-term fulfillment. As we discussed in chapter one, prophecies of this nature were (and are still not) uncommon.

Indeed, His followers began to experience the real fulfillment of His words within "this generation" sooner than they could have expected. In fact the first of these occurred just a few days after Jesus died. His disciples were given clear instructions to go to Galilee, and we read:

Matthew 28:16-18
The eleven disciples went to Galilee, to the mountain to which Jesus had directed them. And when they saw him they worshipped him; but some doubted. And Jesus came and said to them, 'All authority in heaven and on earth has been given to me'.

Thinking him dead and buried they saw him again. He was, as He said He would be, in their midst. Mark records, "The Lord Jesus, after he had spoken to them, was taken up into heaven" (Mark 16:19). Luke says, "He parted from them, and was carried up into heaven. And they [worshipped him] and returned to Jerusalem with great joy" (Luke 24:51,52).

As if to prove the point that this was a two-part prophecy we read these words:

Acts 1:9-11
And when he had said this, as they were looking on, he was lifted up, and a cloud took him out of their sight. And while they were gazing into heaven as he went, behold, two men stood by them in white robes, and said, 'Men of Galilee, why do you stand looking into heaven? This Jesus, who was taken up from you into heaven, will come in the same way as you saw him go into heaven.'

Jesus had died, and the disciples saw Him raised again just as He had promised. Part two is now explained; just as the disciples watched Jesus go into heaven so, in the same way He will return. The angels this time did not say that these disciples would be physically alive to see this happen.

Just thirty-three years later, after the Judean rebellion of 66AD, the Roman Empire led by Emperor Titus massacred thousands of Jewish people and destroyed Jerusalem and its second Temple in

70AD. Many of the survivors were mercilessly taken captive as slaves to Rome whilst others fled to the mountains and countryside. Again this event not only fulfilled the prophecy of Old Testament prophets but also part of that given by Jesus.

To this day our Jewish friends mourn the destruction of the Temple in the annual *Tisha B'Av* (ninth day of the Hebrew month of Av) fast. Interestingly, as if to make a powerful point, although about six hundred and fifty-five years separated the utter destruction of the two Temples they were both made desolate on the anniversary of the same Hebrew calendar date.

The last ignominy befell the remaining rebellious Jewish people led by Simon bar Kokhba, a rebel messiah (leader) who led many astray, when their revolt in 135AD sealed the Jewish fate and dispersed the remaining Jewish nationals.

The promised homeland was completely ploughed and the foundations of the Temple removed. The 'promised' land fell into desolation. During their time of 'exile' the Jewish people were totally scattered across the world in undeniable fulfillment of Leviticus 26:33:

> *I will scatter you among the nations, and I will unsheathe the sword after you; and your land shall be a desolation, and your cities shall be a waste.*

The Jewish people continued to suffer persecution but amazingly they remained a uniquely identifiable group in whatever foreign area and land they resided.

As predicted, the 'great' nation of Israel was sorely punished for disobeying God and for its idolatry. Ezekiel received this message:

Ezekiel 36:17-19

Son of man, when the house of Israel dwelt in their own land, they defiled it by their ways and their doings; their conduct before me was like the uncleanness of a woman in her impurity. So I poured out my wrath upon them for the blood, which they had shed in the land, for the idols with which they had defiled it. I scattered them among the nations, and they were dispersed through the countries; in accordance with their conduct and their deeds I judged them.

I pray that the heart of love and God's infinite grace and mercy will shine brightly as we explore together what God is saying in these last days.

So let's begin with the words of Jesus that we looked at in chapter one:

> **Matthew 24:32,33**
> *From the fig tree learn its lesson: as soon as its branch becomes tender and puts forth its leaves, you know that summer is near. So also, when you see all of these things, you know that he is near; at the very gates.*

What does Jesus mean when He says learn from the fig tree? And what does all this have to do with an event that took place some nineteen hundred years later in May 1948?

The fig tree lesson

The Bible mentions figs and the fig tree on many occasions from the Old Testament book of Genesis where Adam and Eve used its leaves to cover themselves (Genesis 3:7) through to the New Testament book of Revelation where we read about the sixth seal and the heavenly signs (Revelation 6:13).

We also find the fig tree and its fruit mentioned for its deliciousness (Judges 9:11 and Hosea 9:10). On another occasion we find it used as a symbol of prosperity and safety (1 Kings 4:25) and on yet another occasion as part of a pruning parable (Luke 13:6-9). It is a tree that symbolizes the chosen nation of Israel – a nation that has been heavily pruned, cut down, nurtured and watered by God to produce new leaves and fruit. This 'tree' will blossom and bear fruit to the glory of God.

Jesus said that we should look for the new branches and leaves sprouting. In other words, we should watch for and be aware of the signs coming from Israel combining with the other signs mentioned by Jesus.

In May 1948 Israel was reborn; the 'fig tree' began to bud. Jesus said the generation that sees the fig tree leaves sprouting would not pass away until "he is near, at the very gates" and "all these things take place" (Matthew 24:32-34). It is not my place to speculate when the 'generation' began, exactly how long a generation spans or try to predict dates of the second coming. These are in God's hands. What we do know is that prophecies are being fulfilled, and we must keep alert, watch and learn from the Jewish people, who take very seriously their chosen identity with God.

As we have seen, Jesus said, "From the fig tree learn its lesson" (Matthew 24:32). The Greek word for learn is *manthano* meaning 'increase in knowledge, hear and be appraised or fully informed'. Jesus is making the point that we should never be completely ignorant about spiritual or godly signs, events and happenings. We should always be fully informed, alert and aware. There are many lessons that we can learn from Israel.

When we see Bible prophecy being fulfilled and certain things happening they are signs or confirmations of things predicted and to come. They are confirmations of the truthfulness and reliability of God's word and His supernatural Being. They also serve as reminders and warnings of failing to heed what God has to say.

Just as the fig tree sprouting leaves is a sign that summer is approaching so Jesus said, "When you see all these things, you know that he is near, at the very gates" (Matthew 24:33).

What are "all these things" that Jesus refers to? In order to answer this question we need to backtrack to the beginning of the twenty-fourth chapter of Matthew and understand a little about what has become known as the Olivet discourse, which in its entirety covers Matthew chapters 23-25, Mark chapter 13 and Luke chapter 21.

We join the course of events when Jesus was sitting on the Mount of Olives and His disciples came to Him and asked three very important questions. In order to put this in context these questions arose out of the lament of Jesus over Jerusalem and His latter words, "I tell you, you will not see me again, until you say, 'Blessed is he who comes in the name of the Lord.'" (Matthew 23:39). And speaking of the Temple Jesus had said, "There will not be left here one stone upon another, that will not be thrown down" (Matthew 24:2).

The questions and the responses that Jesus gave were not just relevant to His disciples but they are also important to us today. Let's discover why by looking at each of these questions in a little more detail.

The three questions were:

- When will this be (referring to the Temple destruction)?
- What will be the sign of your coming?
- [What will be the sign of the] close of the age (the *parousia*)?

Many Bible scholars actually combine the sign of Jesus' return with the close of the age, and in many ways this makes sense. I do not claim theologian or Bible scholarship, in fact far from it. But for our purposes here I have separated these to first highlight the early signs of the coming and second the impending signs of the end of the age.

The responses that Jesus gave to the disciples' questions are found in the following scriptures from Matthew 24:4-14 where He identified nine signs or warnings that point to the eventual end of the age:

VERSE 5

> Matthew 24:5
> *Many will come in my name, saying, 'I am the Christ,' and they will lead many astray.*

The Hebrew word for Christ used in this verse is messiah or more accurately *meshiahh* meaning 'to smear' or, as Jeremiah used it, 'to paint' (Jeremiah 22:14). Shepherds used to carry a flask of olive oil, which was typically used for cooking, as a medicine and even a disinfectant smeared or painted over an injury to the shepherd or sheep. In Exodus 29:7 we learn that the oil was also used as an anointing:

> *Take the anointing oil, and pour it on his head and anoint him.*

Having established an Old Testament Hebraic link with the word *messiah*, a term incidentally used twice by John (1:41 and 4:25), the 'anointing' theme continues through the Greek word for *messiah*, which is *christos* meaning 'the anointed one'. When used in its widest sense the term *messiah* refers to a leader of a cause. Jesus predicted something of what the disciples would themselves experience after His death. The Bible specifically mentions three leaders who led many astray. In Acts chapter five we read of the first two bellicose Jewish leaders of a cause:

- Theudas (approximately 45AD):

Acts 5:36
[He] arose, giving himself out to be somebody, and a number of men, about four hundred, joined him; but he was slain and all who followed him were dispersed and came to nothing.

- Judas the Galilean:

Acts 5:37
[He] arose in the days of the census and drew away some of the people after him; he also perished, and all who followed him were scattered.

Following these accounts we read:

Acts 5:38,39
So in the present case I tell you, keep away from these men and let them alone; for if this plan or this undertaking is of men, it will fail; but if it is of God, you will not be able to overthrow them. You might even be found opposing God!

Our third example is found in Acts chapter twenty-one.

- An unnamed Egyptian (approximately 54AD)

When Paul was arrested following a misunderstanding and a mob attack he spoke to the tribune in Greek. The surprised commander said:

Acts 21:38
Are you not the Egyptian, then, who recently stirred up a revolt and led the four thousand men of the Assassins out into the wilderness?

Paul had been mistaken as a rebel leader.

Although not attributed to anyone in particular we also read about concerns arising somewhere between the periods of the three rebel leaders mentioned above affecting the church. Paul writes:

Galatians 1:6,7
I am astonished that you are so quickly deserting him who called you in the grace of Christ and turning to a different gospel – not that there is another gospel, but there are those some who trouble you and want to pervert the gospel of Christ.

Galatians 3:1
O foolish Galatians! Who has bewitched you?

In summary, within a very short period after the death of Jesus each of His disciples began to see something of what He was speaking about with regard to false messiahs. Since the nineteenth century we have had at least forty claims[14] from people calling themselves the Son of God, the messiah or similar.

VERSE 6

Matthew 24:6
You will hear of wars and rumours of wars.

Wars have of course occurred since time began. In 40AD the anti-Jewish Roman Emperor Caligula tried to put a statue of himself in the Temple in Jerusalem. This led to a Jewish-Roman war. A number of revolts followed across the Empire, and so Claudius, who had succeeded the assassinated Caligula, allowed the Jewish people to practise their religion and so maintain peace. By 66AD and the reign of Nero, Jewish-Roman relations worsened, and a series of further revolts arose.

Interestingly, moving to modern history, there have been about one hundred and thirty wars spread across the world even since the end of the Second World War!

All of this seems disastrous, but Jesus said, "See that you are not alarmed; for this must take place, but the end is not yet" (Matthew 24:6).

VERSE 7A

Matthew 24:7a
Nation will rise against nation, and kingdom against kingdom.

Apart from the Jewish-Roman wars and many since, perhaps the most dramatic of these occurred during the First World War in which an estimated twenty million people were needlessly killed and the Second World War in which over three times more deaths took place than during the First World War. There has not been one year since the end of the Second World War where a war somewhere in the world has not taken place. There have been an increasing number of nation wars or threats in the twentieth and twenty-first centuries.

---

[14] *en.wikipedia.org/wiki/Messiah_claimants*

VERSE 7B

Matthew 24:7b
There will be famines and earthquakes in various places.

Matthew records that there was an earthquake when Jesus died. The number of major earthquakes worldwide is so many that it is difficult to keep up with these, but a conservative estimate is twenty thousand per year.

Agabus, led by the Spirit, foretold a world famine, which took place during the time of Claudius who reigned during 41-54AD. We read:

Acts 11:28-30
The disciples determined, every one according to his ability, to send relief to the brethren who lived in Judea; and they did so, sending it to the elders by the hand of Barnabas and Saul.

The world has not been short of famines. Since the time of Jesus there have been well over one hundred and fifty major famines worldwide. During the Middle Ages there were also ninety-five famines in Britain.

Devastation caused by pointless revolts, wars, earthquakes and famines have led to millions of deaths, but Jesus said, "All this is but the beginning of the birth-pangs" (Matthew 24:8).

VERSE 9

Matthew24:9
They will deliver you up to tribulation, and put you to death; and you will be hated by all nations for my name's sake.

We know from scripture that Stephen was brutally martyred very shortly after the death of Jesus, probably in or around 34AD, because he spoke boldly about His death and resurrection. We read:

Acts 6:8-10
Stephen, full of grace and power, did great wonders and signs among the people. Then some of those who belonged to the synagogue of the Freedmen (as it was called), and of the Cyrenians, and of the Alexandrians, and of those from Cilicia and Asia, arose and disputed with Stephen. But they could not withstand the wisdom and the Spirit with which he spoke.

The shocking immaturity of man who could not get his way and whose pride had been hurt led to another innocent death.

In Acts chapter twelve we read of another disciple, James, who was also martyred, in about 41AD by King Herod (Agrippa I) who at the same time also imprisoned Peter.

> **Acts 12:1-3**
> *Herod the king laid violent hands upon some who belonged to the church. He killed James the brother of John with the sword; and when he saw that it pleased the Jews, he proceeded to arrest Peter.*

In about 64AD many Christians were both persecuted and killed by the Romans under Nero, and we also know that Peter (and many also believe Paul) was martyred. Concerning Paul, we really do not know about his death; the Bible does not give us any information.

Christian martyrdom has taken place since the birth of the New Testament Church. Across the world even today there are literally thousands of Christians martyred for their faith each year.

VERSE 10

> **Matthew 24:10**
> *Many will fall away and betray one another, and hate one another.*

This is something that has taken place since early Christian Church times. Today as we look around at the state of the Church, time spent in prayer has all but disappeared, sermons are shockingly watered down and humanism has been enthusiastically embraced. Many want to hear about prosperity and the 'love' gospel.[15] God is effectively 'tolerated' in churches steeped in tradition and secularism.

Christian believers will argue against one another over man-introduced philosophies and theologies – arguments that will demonstrate a lack of time spent with God and the Holy Spirit in the scriptures; arguments that will carry with them the subtle deceptions of Satan fed into hearts of unbelief and pride.

---

[15] See Appendix II

VERSE 11

Matthew 24:11
Many false prophets will arise and lead many astray.

Just as scripture has said, over the centuries many false prophets have been (and are being) identified and revealed.

VERSE 12

Matthew 24:12
Because wickedness is multiplied most men's love will grow cold.

This is a point made earlier in this chapter when discussing the state of our churches.

VERSE 13

Matthew 24:13
This gospel of the kingdom will be preached throughout the whole world.

Certainly the disciples and apostles went out and preached the gospel to the 'known' world. Missionaries and evangelists have taken the gospel to all parts of the globe.

Jesus then turns His attention to the prophecies found in Daniel (chapters 9-12 particularly contain end time prophecies) and talks about the great tribulation and His return.

As we have discovered, the disciples of Jesus did actually experience and meet head-on those things that Jesus prophesied as they occurred at their early stages. Successive generations have also experienced these things, and we continue to go through these today in a global and heightened way. But something highly significant changed in 1948.

Why is May 1948 important?

For over two thousand years the Jewish people had been dispersed – unrecognized as a nation in their own right. However, this all changed in just one remarkable day in May 1948, which in itself fulfilled the prophecy declared by Isaiah:

Isaiah 66:7,8

Before she was in labour she gave birth; before her pain came upon her she was delivered of a son. Who has heard of such a thing? Who has seen such things? Shall a land be born in one day? Shall a nation be brought forth in one moment? For as soon as Zion was in labour she brought forth her sons.

Many Jewish people spent years praying for the re-gathering of their nation, but they remained in unbelief; they did not, and many still do not, recognize Jesus as God's son, Yeshua the Messiah.

It was in May 1948 that the Polish-born Zionist leader David Ben-Gurion (1886-1973) became the first Prime Minister of the newly formed Independent State of Israel (known in Hebrew as *Medinat Yisrael*). On the afternoon of Friday 14th May, 1948, at 4pm, Jewish leaders (or perhaps more appropriately we should call them the Founding Fathers of modern-day Israel) met at the Tel Aviv museum of Arts to sign the Israeli Declaration of Independence.

Following the reading of the declaration that contained these words...

This right is the natural right of the Jewish people to be masters of their own fate, like all other nations, in their own sovereign State.[16]

...Rabbi Fishman Maimon (born Yehuda Leib Fishman 1875-1962), who had helped to draft the eventual Declaration of Independence, recited the *shehechiyanu,* a Jewish prayer of thanksgiving and blessing that thanks God for sustaining their lives and bringing them to times of joyfulness. The prayer is a reminder that God gives life, and it appropriately recognizes that God should receive glory for the good that comes upon His people. The words of the *shehechiyanu* are:

Blessed are You, Lord our God, King of the universe, who has kept us alive, and sustained us, and enabled us to reach this moment.[17]

This significant historic occasion fulfilled a major Bible prophecy. I highlighted this prophecy from the Old Testament book of Ezekiel

---

[16] The Israeli Declaration of Independence 1948

[17] Hebrew: *Baruch Atah Adonai Eloheinu Melech Ha-Olam Shehehchiyahnu vekiyamanu vehegianu lazman ha-zeh*

at the head of this chapter, but for continuity and ease I have copied it here:

Ezekiel 37:21,22

Thus says the Lord God: Behold, I will take the people of Israel from the nations among which they have gone, and will gather them from all sides, and bring them to their own land; and I will make them one nation in the land, upon the mountains of Israel; and one king shall be king over them all; and they shall be no longer two nations, and no longer divided into two kingdoms.

May 1948 saw the eventual fulfillment of this prophecy.

What we should understand is that the fulfilling of this prophecy represents the turning point toward the end days and the return of Jesus – a 'speeding up' of God's end time plan that is gathering momentum. In short, time for procrastination, complacency, misunderstanding and unbelief has run out. Neither Jewish nor Gentile people can continue to sit back and wait.

I've heard it before

At this point, it is helpful to digress from our thoughts about the events of 1948 to look at what underlies the fulfilling of this Bible prophecy. There are words that I have heard many times, and they sadden me every time to hear them, namely, "We have been talking about the return of Christ and the end of the age for centuries. Generation upon generation thought that they were living in the last days. Generation upon generation thought that Jesus would return in their lifetime. It hasn't happened!" If these are words that you have used or think deep down then you are in a very precarious situation.

The point being expressed by these people is undeniably true. But complacency and failing to take note of God's prophetic signs may well prove costly and even disastrous. The parable of the ten maidens in Matthew 25:1-13 tells us that we must watch, be ready and prepare for the return of Jesus. The unwise missed out!

I do not know about you but I do not want to find myself counted among the unwise. In his second letter Peter talks about the second coming, and he says a few things that should make us re-think our laissez-faire attitudes:

2 Peter 3:9-13

The Lord is not slow about his promise as some count slowness, but is forbearing toward you, not wishing that any should perish, but that all should reach repentance. [Repentance is the only way in which we can deal with sin in our lives. It is part of getting ready for Jesus to return.] But the day of the Lord will come like a thief, and then the heavens will pass away with a loud noise, and the elements will be dissolved with fire, and the earth and the works that are upon it will be burned up. Since all these things are thus to be dissolved, what sort of persons ought you to be in lives of holiness and godliness, waiting for a hastening the coming of the day of God, because of which the heavens will be kindled and dissolved, and the elements will melt with fire! But according to his promise we wait for new heavens and a new earth in which righteousness dwells.

What we are seeing here is that God is patiently waiting for as many people as possible to repent. We, the Church, are solemnly charged with the God-given responsibility of preaching the gospel throughout the world. There is however a caution in Peter's words wrapped up in the form of "but": the return of Jesus will come suddenly.

Peter then poses the question, "What sort of persons ought you [we] to be?" The only answer is that it is necessary for the pure quality of our character to display holy conduct and reverence to God. In other words, when Jesus returns this is what He will be looking for from us. Everything about us will be 'burned' in God's refinery, and we must ultimately be found righteous and without blemish. It is for these reasons that Peter then goes on to say:

2 Peter 3:14,15

Since you wait for these, be zealous to be found by him without spot or blemish, and at peace. And count the forbearance of the Lord as salvation.

Wow, what a statement: "...be zealous ... be found by him without spot or blemish ... at peace." Many Christians have thought that they can just sit back – it does not matter and all is well – believing that when Jesus returns they will be okay. It's only the unsaved that have to look out, isn't it? Yes, they have to come to repentance, but those who are Christian believers are also expected to zealously seek holiness and count this time as fulfilling their salvation

– guarding it with every fibre of their being. In the New Testament book of Hebrews we read:

Hebrews 3:12
Take care brethren, lest there be in any of you an evil, unbelieving heart, leading you to fall away from the living God.

Put another way, we have to make sure that 'our house' is in order and leave nothing to chance. A heart of unbelief is evil in God's eyes.

It may have all been said before. We may have heard it before. Generations before us may have expected Jesus to return. Who knows, generations after us may do the same. But let us be found worthy. Jesus actually put it this way:

Luke 21:36
Watch at all times, praying that you may have strength to escape all these things that will take place, and to stand before the Son of man.

The events of 1948 are highly significant. The fig tree has most certainly sprouted. To clarify this still further, let's take a look at some of the events leading to our present historical position.

As we have already discovered, the Old Testament book of Ezekiel, in chapters 36 and 37, foretold the restoration of Israel and the re-gathering of the Jewish people from all corners of the world to form an independent nation. From 1948 the following prophecy was fulfilled:

Ezekiel 36:33-36
Thus says the Lord God: On the day that I cleanse you from all your iniquities, I will cause the cities to be inhabited, and the waste places shall be rebuilt. And the land that was desolate shall be tilled, instead of being the desolation that it was in the sight of all who passed by. And they will say, 'This land that was desolate has become like the Garden of Eden; and the waste and desolate and ruined cities are now inhabited and fortified.' Then the nations that are left round about you shall know that I, the Lord, have rebuilt the ruined places, and replanted that which was desolate; I, the Lord, have spoken, and I will do it.

The Satanic atrocities of 1939-1945, which attempted to wipe out the Jewish people and prevent *Eretz-Israel* (Hebrew for 'the Land of Israel') from being re-established, failed. Even on the following day that the Declaration was finally signed, Egypt, Jordan, Lebanon and Syria attacked the new country and a battle (which became known as the War of Independence, lasting fifteen months) took place. If Israel had lost this battle her fate may have been tragically sealed, but God was watching over His people and the onslaught failed. God was true to His word: "I, the Lord, have spoken, and I will do it" (Ezekiel 36:36).

The fact that Israel defeated Egypt, Jordan, Lebanon and Syria was not only an unprecedented and fearsome shock to them but it came against the odds. To underestimate this victory would be folly to the extreme. God said, "I will do it," and He did.

Moving forward to 1967 yet another significant war took place. The Six Day War (known in Hebrew as *Mil'hement sheshet Hayamim*) initiated by Egypt, Jordan and Syria, who were still hurting from what they called the 'shame' of the 1948 conflict, began on 5th June and ended on 10th June, 1967. Israel once again emerged victorious gaining the Gaza Strip from Egypt, Golan Heights from Syria, East Jerusalem from Jordan, the Sinai Peninsular from Egypt and the West Bank from Jordan.

The miracle of the Six Day War should post a warning to all would-be invaders or antagonists no matter how powerful they think they are – but we will learn later that this warning message has not been learnt. God has posted His warning and proved His power. He will triumph again.

If anyone wanted proof of God's promises and abilities to fulfill His word then these should surely be proof enough. Paul's words to the Roman house churches tells us as Christian believers all we need to know:

Romans 8:28-31
In everything God works for good with those who love him, who are called according to his purpose. For those whom he foreknew he also predestined to be conformed to the image of his Son, in order that he might be the first-born among many brethren. And those whom he predestined he also called; and those whom he called he also justified; and those whom he justified he also glorified. What then shall we say to this? If God is for us, who is against us?

What a faithful and mighty God we have!

It should come as no surprise to us to learn that David Ben-Gurion was openly recognized as one of Time Magazine's one hundred most influential people of the twentieth century. The miracle of Israel being reborn as a nation came about against great odds and terrible suffering.

In summary, 1948 signified the birth contractions, the early stages of the birth of the last days. Jesus left us with this warning:

> Matthew 24:32,33
> *From the fig tree learn its lesson: as soon as its branch becomes tender and puts forth its leaves, you know that summer is near. So also, when you see all these things, you know that he is near, at the very gates.*

I am genuinely shocked and saddened when I come across those who say, "I have heard it before," or, "It has been said by many." It is to our great loss when a self-satisfied, smug and unconcerned attitude prevents us from seeking more from God. I am not talking here of seeking more at a superficial level but rather of seeking more from heaven itself: miracles, healings, signs and wonders as everyday happenings; being dissatisfied with anything less than God's supernatural best. We are in the last days. This generation is ripe for the swift fulfillment of the remaining prophecies. Jesus is coming back and we must prepare ourselves.

If the Jewish people remained in unbelief, were disobedience and therefore serving inadequately, a logical question is, "Why were Bible prophecies about Israel becoming a nation again in its own right fulfilled?" To help us with this question Ezekiel said:

> Ezekiel 36:22-24
> *Thus says the Lord God: it is not for your sake, O house of Israel, that I am about to act, but for the sake of my holy name, which you have profaned among the nations to which you came. And I will vindicate the holiness of my great name, which has been profaned among them; and the nations will know that I am the Lord, says the Lord God, when through you I vindicate my holiness before their eyes.*

God has miraculously vindicated His holy name. The evidence is plain to see – but how has the world reacted? Almost predictably it has largely ignored this and many other Bible prophecies. It has generally continued to ignore God and Jesus. Dear friend, we cannot continue to ignore God, Jesus and what is happening in Israel. What happens in Israel and Jerusalem cannot be isolated and separated from the impact that this will have and does have on both the Church and world as a whole.

> **John 13:19**
> *I tell you this now, before it takes place, that when it does take place you may believe that I am he.*

CHAPTER THREE

The Peace of Jerusalem

Psalm 122:6,7
Pray for the peace of Jerusalem! 'May they prosper who love you! Peace be within your walls, and security within your towers!'

Seed thought

No city in the world, not even Athens or Rome, ever played as great a role in the life of a nation for so long a time, as Jerusalem has done in the life of the Jewish people.

- David Ben-Gurion[18]

Introduction

The unique city of Jerusalem and its Temple have a special place in the eyes of God who said:

Genesis 12:3
I will bless those who bless you, and him who curses you I will curse; and by you all the families of the earth shall bless themselves.

These are extremely strong and powerful words. These are words so potent that we would probably say today 'they mean business'. They are words that cannot be ignored or trifled with. In just a short, simple sentence God makes His point very clear: the attitude that a

---

[18] *www.jewish-wisdom.com/index.php?submit=author&a=David+Ben-Gurion*

person has toward Jerusalem will mirror the attitude that God will have toward them. Bless Jerusalem and receive abundance from God. Curse Jerusalem and be cursed and destitute.

We are instructed:

Psalm 122:6-9
Pray for the peace of Jerusalem! 'May they prosper who love you! Peace be within your walls, and security within your towers!' For my brethren and companions' sake I will say, 'Peace be within you!' For the sake of the house of the Lord our God, I will seek your good.

This verse says that those who pray for and love Jerusalem will prosper. The Hebrew word used for prosper is *shalah* meaning 'be at ease, at rest, quiet or tranquil'. It is clear that *shalah* is not offering a promise of financial prosperity, as some have believed or pedaled to encourage giving financially to the work in Israel or any other related cause. It is about maintaining our relational ease and tranquility before God.

Please do not misunderstand – the point is not that we should stop giving financial blessing to the work of bringing our Jewish friends in Israel to enlightenment about the true identity of Jesus (Yeshua). Far, far from it! But rather, our incentive should be to freely and lovingly recognize God's chosen people and obey God's words free of any notion of a possible benefit to us personally. If giving money is what we wish to do, it is a matter between God and us. The act of giving should come from a heart of obedience and love, not for what may eventually be gained or what we hope to gain for our personal benefit, whatever that may be.

Paul said (as we too should say), "My heart's desire and prayer to God for them is that they may be saved. I bear them witness that they have a zeal for God, but it is not enlightened" (Romans 10:1,2). We are to bless, be thankful to and pray for enlightenment to come to our Jewish friends. We are to love them and show them our relationship with God and, as Paul said, "make Israel jealous" (Romans 11:11) – stir them to find Jesus and to pray for peace in Jerusalem.

The Christian church has been guilty of being somewhat haughty toward the Jewish people. Jesus warned about sitting in judgment over others whilst we ourselves are just as guilty. Let's take a moment to consider these words:

Matthew 7:2,3

For with the judgment you pronounce you will be judged, and the measure you give will be the measure you get. Why do you see the speck that is in your brother's eye, but do not notice the log that is in your own eye?

Let's not be found as hypocrites. Rather let each of us be thankful for and love the Jewish people into the kingdom of God. This is a people who have suffered many atrocities. Despite all, they have not stopped pursuing God.

What does the peace of Jerusalem mean?

We are, as it says in the Hebrew language, to *"Sha-alu Shalowm Yirushalayim"*, which roughly translated means, "Pray for peace in Jerusalem." The peace that this is talking about is not simply a period of respite from war and conflict. The Hebrew word *shalowm* means to be 'complete, whole, content, sound and tranquil' or 'at peaceful ease with God'. It is about being in covenant relationship with Him. It is about the Jewish nation being reconciled with their Messiah.

One of the most heart-wrenching scenes in the New Testament Gospels is found in Luke, who wrote:

Luke 19:41-44

When he drew near and saw the city he wept over it, saying, 'Would that even today you knew the things that make for peace! But now they are hid from your eyes. For the days shall come upon you, when your enemies will cast up a bank about you and surround you, and hem you in on every side, and dash you to the ground, you and your children within you, and they will not leave one stone upon another in you; because you did not know the time of your visitation.'

Jesus had come to His people. In these few words He was expressing both His and His Father's love for the Jewish people. He lived among them and demonstrated signs to demonstrate who He really was, but the people, not knowing what they had done, rejected Him.

The words found in John's Gospel suddenly ring starkly and dramatically clear: "He came to his own home, and his own people received him not" (John 1:11). I cannot even begin to grasp how heartbreaking this moment must have been for Jesus. His own beloved people rejected Him. Those of us who know what the loneliness of rejection is like will have but a taste of the pain Jesus went through.

When we look at the Greek word translated as 'wept' we find the word *klaio*, which means 'to mourn, to weep as one in pain and grief'. It is that type of weeping that is uncontrollable, deep and audible. It is literally 'to break down in tears'. This was more than a few tears coming to the eyes or even tears rolling down the cheeks. This was pain and grief coming from the heart and soul.

This picture of Jesus weeping uncontrollably over Jerusalem, His own people, also has a second aspect to it. The picture that we are seeing conveys how much love Jesus has for *all* sinners, for every one of us. We are in the heart of Jesus, whether Jewish or Gentile.

If we are really honest, there has been a certain lack of ease, even arrogance and ignorance, displayed by many Christians toward the Jewish people in thinking that we have got it right with Jesus and God. Some have even either criticized or shown jealousy toward the Jewish people because God has favoured and blessed them despite the fact that they have often not deserved special treatment. When we honestly look at the state of the Church today it is quite obvious that Christian believers have little to boast about.

Jewish-Christian relationship

It would probably be true to say that most Jewish people characterize a Christian differently from the way a Christian would describe themself. And many Christians would equally characterize a Jewish person differently. These differences account for a great deal of misunderstanding and misrepresentation.

Many Jewish people have a generic understanding of what a Christian is. They would not necessarily understand denominational differences or distinguish between a Christian believer, the Christian church and a Christian nation. These are, after all, areas of misunderstanding even among those who would categorize themselves as belonging to one or more of these categories.

Christians similarly will typically misunderstand what a Jewish person really is. Christians will not understand or be able to distinguish between different Jewish movements, Jewish people born in different countries and the different beliefs.

Many have reached a point where much of what they say about one another, whether out of ignorance, misunderstanding, pride or poor teaching, is actually untrue. When we engage in these arguments and disagreements we break the Ninth Commandment: "You shall not bear false witness against your neighbour" (Exodus 20:16). A degree of fault lies on both sides, but the born again Christian has a divine responsibility to rightly handle the word of God and preach the gospel of Christ in love and humility.

Many Christians do not take heed of, or attempt to understand, Jewish worship and commitments and so we lose much of the significance and richness of our relationship with God. This attitude seems to forget Paul's words as a Jewish person:

> Romans 1:16
> *I am not ashamed of the gospel: it is the power of God for salvation to every one who has faith, to the Jew first and also to the Greek [Gentile].*

> Romans 2:9
> *For God shows no partiality.*

Jesus was himself Jewish and His message was first brought to the Jewish people, but because of the cross all are now included in the gospel. Before any of us point a finger let us never forget that not one of us deserve God's love, grace and mercy.

Yes, the Jewish people as a whole originally rejected Jesus, and this opened the door so that the cross unifies us. The covenants that Abraham, Isaac and Jacob received for the Jewish people became ours through Jesus. This claim is based upon Paul's words, writing to the Ephesians, when he gave this reminder to the Gentiles:

> Ephesians 2:11-13
> *Remember that at one time you Gentiles in the flesh, called the uncircumcision by what is called the circumcision, which is made in the flesh by hands – remember that you were at that time separate from Christ, alienated from the commonwealth of Israel, and strangers to the covenants of promise, having no hope and without God in the world. But now in Christ Jesus you who were once far off have been brought near in the blood of Christ.*

It would be true to say that originally there was a division: the Jewish people and the Gentiles. God chose the Jewish people, saying, "You shall be holy to me; for I the Lord am holy, and have separated you from the peoples, that you should be mine" (Leviticus 20:26). This statement from God is no less true today than it was when God first made it. There are still divisions today but they are of our making: the Jewish people to whom God said, "You are mine"; the Christian believers, the true Church brought to God through the blood of Christ; and those who do not fall into the first two categories and choose to stay outside, the non-believing Gentiles.

Paul summarizes what I am trying to say in the words quoted earlier, "God shows no partiality" (Romans 2:9). The 'bottom line' is that no arrogance, mistrust or misunderstanding between the Jewish people and the true Christian believer should exist.

These opening thoughts leave us with two important questions:

- Why is Jerusalem important?
- Why is praying for the peace of Jerusalem important?

Before we tackle the story of Jerusalem and why it is important, let's first understand why I am taking time to trace some of the history; and why we as Christian believers need to learn about and ally ourselves with the Jewish people and Jerusalem.

For far too long Gentile Christian believers have largely ignored, or been ignorant of, the vital importance of the Jewish people, their significant biblical worship roots and the true value of Jerusalem. Most of this has come about because of poor teaching or, as it has been in my personal experience, a total absence of teaching. Dear reader, I don't know how to express this adequately, but we cannot continue to live in such poor relationship and understanding. Writing to the Roman house churches Paul quoted from Hosea saying:

Romans 9:25,26
Those who were not my people I will call 'my people', and her who was not beloved I will call 'my beloved.' 'And in the very place where it was said to them, 'you are not my people,' they will be called 'sons of the living God'.

We owe a great deal to a people who have not always got it right with God but have faithfully preserved His word, the scriptures. But why Jerusalem?

Why is Jerusalem important?

In order to help us with this question let's take a prayerful look at the following Bible statements:

Deuteronomy 11:11,12
The land which you are going over to possess is a land of hills and valleys, which drinks water by the rain from heaven, a land which the Lord your God cares for; the eyes of the Lord your God are always upon it, from the beginning of the year to the end of the year.

(It is worth noting that although Jerusalem has suffered food shortages during the course of its long history it has never lacked water.)

1 Kings 9:3
I have heard your prayer and your supplication, which you have made before me; I have consecrated this house which you have built, and put my name there for ever; my eyes and my heart will be there for all time.

Jeremiah 3:17
Jerusalem shall be called the throne of the Lord, and all nations shall gather to it, to the presence of the Lord in Jerusalem, and they shall no more stubbornly follow their own evil heart.

Zechariah 1:14-16
Thus says the Lord of hosts: I am exceedingly jealous for Jerusalem and for Zion. And I am very angry with the nations that are at ease; for while I was angry but a little they furthered the disaster. Therefore, thus says the Lord, I have returned to Jerusalem with compassion; my house shall be built in it, says the Lord of hosts, and the measuring line shall be stretched out over Jerusalem.

These four scripture examples tell us quite simply that God has chosen the land, Jerusalem and its Temple. In another words, Jerusalem is His chosen place of dwelling and His place of judgment. It is this small city that Jesus wept over. It is from here that Jesus was eventually taken into heaven, and it is here where His feet will come and stand on the day He returns. These facts alone should give us a clue about why Jerusalem is so important. But let's take a look at some of its troubled history, its amazing journey of suffering and, against incredible odds, how it has survived.

This is truly a story of God in action – God proving who He is through the life of His chosen people. The fact is biblical Judaism and Christianity should, and one day will, unify. Although the ministry of Jesus was essentially to his Jewish neighbours He was the perfect embodiment of this unification. The exciting thing today is that God is hastening the call for Messianic Jews and true Christian Gentile believers to get back to basics, to return to their roots. God made a precious covenant with Abraham, and Jesus extended this covenant to the Gentiles through faith in him, and so both are inextricably included in God's perfect plan and the wonderful recognition as "sons of the living God" (Romans 9:26). The church has not taken the place of the Jewish people and promises made to them. It has become a part of it.

When, as Christian believers, we want to understand scripture in its deepest sense, what do we do? We trace the original Hebrew meanings, the original Jewish holy practices and feasts, etc. Why? Because these are our roots. Jesus was born Jewish, and to understand Him we need to understand His background. Paul, who born Jewish, devoted his ministry to the Gentiles, bridging the gap between the two.

I hope and pray that these observations will whet your appetite to know more and to seek God's heart and purposes in these matters. So let's take a look at how God has always remained true and faithful to His promises.

The rise, fall and rise of Jerusalem

In order to help us understand the astonishing story of Jerusalem and its Jewish people, who are inextricably linked to the city, we will need to take a very brief look at just some of the ups and downs of its history. It is not possible in the context of this book to look at the finer details or cover every aspect. But as we sample the amazing resilience of the Jewish nation and the holy city, it is important for us to keep in the forefront of our mind that although this city, perhaps like no other, has seen more than its fair share of conflict, it is, as we read in 1 Kings, God's chosen city:

1 Kings 11:13
I will give one tribe to your son, for the sake of David my servant and for the sake of Jerusalem which I have chosen.

The Psalmist also said:

Psalm 76:1,2
In Judah God is known; his name is great in Israel. His abode has been established in Salem, his dwelling place in Zion.

Jerusalem is one of the world's oldest cities, and during its tumultuous history it has, to date, been destroyed twice, besieged about twenty-three times, further attacked about twenty-five times and captured or recaptured well over forty times. The Bible tells us that much of this turbulence is a direct consequence of the disobedience of God's chosen people and God was not 'with' them. The Old Testament book of Leviticus warned about the consequences of disobedience saying, "I will set my face against you" (Leviticus 26:17). Despite this, God has never rescinded His promise or lost His compassion for Jerusalem and His people. Indeed, as if to make the point, scripture is full of examples where the Israelites never lost a battle, even against great odds, when God was with them.

With these opening thoughts in mind let's take a 'whistle stop tour' of the history of Jerusalem. We begin by first learning that the ancient city of Jerusalem has been known by many names, but for our purposes here let's take a look at just some of these names found in scripture:

SALEM[19]

Genesis 14:18
...and Melchizedek king of Salem brought out bread and wine; he was priest of God Most High.

Salem was the name given to the city when Melchizedek ruled it. The name 'Melchizedek' means 'king of righteousness'. The Hebrew word *salem* means 'peace'.

JEBUS

1 Chronicles 11:4
David and all Israel went to Jerusalem, that is Jebus, where the Jebusites were, the inhabitants of the land.

Jebus was the name given to the area where the Jebusites lived.

---

[19] Sometimes written *Shalem*.

MORIAH

> **2 Chronicles 3:1**
> *Solomon began to build the house of the Lord in Jerusalem on Mount Moriah, where the Lord had appeared to David his father, at the place that David had appointed, on the threshing floor of Ornan the Jebusite.*

The name Moriah comes from the original name of the hill country, the mount upon which the Temple was first built.

Other names were given to the city describing its qualities. For example:

HABITATION OF RIGHTEOUSNESS

> **Jeremiah 31:23**
> *The Lord bless you, O habitation of righteousness, O holy hill.*

CITY OF GOD

> **Psalm 87:3**
> *Glorious things are spoken of you, O city of God.*

THE FAITHFUL CITY

> **Zechariah 8:3**
> *I will return to Zion, and dwell in the midst of Jerusalem, and Jerusalem shall be called the faithful city, and the mountain of the Lord of hosts, the holy mountain.*

The Greek word for Jerusalem is *Hierosolyma* meaning 'holy city'. The Hebrew name for Jerusalem is *Yerushalayim* meaning 'God sees or flows complete peace' (we now shorten this to simply 'city of peace'). Jerusalem: a name that means 'city of peace', and yet its history is one of conflict and bloodshed, a history synonymous with the Jewish people and the holy seat of God. These descriptions alone tell us how important this city is for the entire world and especially for us as Christian believers. Nonetheless, let's take a closer look at its story.

Jerusalem is first mentioned in the Bible in a scripture that we have already referred to above (Genesis 14:18): the meeting of Melchizedek and Abraham. We will, however, begin our view of Jerusalem some years into its birth. It was around 1000BC when King David took control of the city and called it 'David'. He began, and his son Solomon completed, the building of the first Jerusalem Temple. This act sealed a national Jewish bond in this area, which lasted for about four hundred years.

Regrettably idol worship took root, and the prophet Jeremiah prophesied the threat posed by the Babylonians as described in Jeremiah chapter 36 – but, sadly, Jehoiakim the king of Judah and the inhabitants of Jerusalem would not heed the warning. In about 587BC the Babylonians, under the reign of Nebuchadnezzar II, eventually conquered the city, pillaged it and destroyed its Temple.

Jeremiah prophesied:

Jeremiah 29:10
When seventy years are completed for Babylon, I will visit you, and I will fulfil to you my promise and bring you back to this place.

Within one hundred years the Jewish people had joyfully made their way back, rebuilt their temple and occupied the city as before. Psalm 126 is in fact a psalm of thanks to God for deliverance, and it expresses the joy of the people, as illustrated in these words:

Psalm 126:1-6
When the Lord restored the fortunes of Zion, we were like those who dream. Then our mouth was filled with laughter, and our tongue with shouts of joy; then they said amongst the nations, 'The Lord has done great things for them.' The Lord has done great things for us; we are glad.

The next five hundred years or so saw the Jewish people clinging to control of Jerusalem despite many attempts to attack and overthrow it or to disrupt its customs and practices.

In 70AD the Romans destroyed the second Temple, and following a series of Jewish revolts the Jewish people were eventually expelled from the land in 135AD. Some Jewish people did however return to the area by the fourth century, and they were eventually permitted to practice various aspects of their religion under Christian rule by the fifth century.

Difficulties arose again when Theodosius II (401-450), otherwise known as Emperor Flavius Theodosius, had all the education funds that had been faithfully collected by the Jewish people paid into his coffers, and later he restricted many of the rights of the Jewish people. This led to only Jewish people being allowed to come to the

Temple once per year. Following a number of successive upheavals over the next couple of centuries a small Jewish community was once again allowed to occupy Jerusalem. Worship in the Temple was re-established in the eighth century.

Unfortunately, yet again peace did not last long, and throughout the ninth to eleventh centuries the fortunes of the small Jewish community went from harsh measures being taken against them by the Fatimid Muslim Dynasty (969AD) through to a revival given to Jerusalem by the Jewish Diaspora (the mourners of Zion who had been dispersed from their homeland) and the resultant increase of communities being established in the area.

The Crusades of the twelfth century saw terrible massacres of the Jewish people, but these resilient people once again survived and began to re-group. Notably in 1211 three hundred rabbis from across Europe returned to Jerusalem. Although various periods of hardship and difficulties again arose, the thirteenth to the nineteenth centuries saw more and more Jewish people being drawn toward, and gradually returning to, Jerusalem and its surrounding 'homeland' areas.

By the late eighteenth and early nineteenth century, immigration of the Jewish people had increased greatly. The Zionist movement (those seeking to create a Jewish state) founded by Theodor Hertzl (1860-1904) was eventually established in 1897. This influx began once again to trouble various nations, especially those surrounding the region and who opposed the Jewish people.

Amidst turmoil in the region and the fall of the Ottoman Empire, what became known as the 'Jerusalem Operations' of 1917 led to the British Empire forces capturing Jerusalem and General Edmund Allenby[20] (1861-1936). This was biblically significant because a 'Christian' had taken control of the city, and this event paved the way to a reuniting of the Jewish people and the Gentiles.

Jerusalem became the capital of Palestine (a name for the region revived from the Crusade period and beyond) in 1923 and until 1948, during which time a number of riots took place. The Second World War saw terrible atrocities inflicted upon the Jewish people through the holocaust in which about six million were slaughtered. Indeed

---

[20] General Allenby was later to become Field Marshal Sir Edmund Allenby in 1919 and later still in the same year Viscount Allenby of Megiddo.

Psalm 102:3 prophesied the holocaust in these words: "My days pass away like smoke, and my bones burn like a furnace" – a stark description of the many Jewish people who were mercilessly placed in the gas ovens and burned. Also, verse seven says, "All the day my enemies taunt me, those who deride me use my name for a curse," which was fulfilled when the Jewish people were forcibly made to wear the Star of David and their homes and businesses painted with the name 'Jew' to signify who lived and worked in certain places.

Paradoxically, whilst all of this was happening, the war helped the Jewish people, and during this period many settled in what was then known as Palestine.

After the Second World War, a Resolution was finally passed by the United Nations General Assembly in 1947 (Resolution 181 [II]) dealing with the future government of Palestine. The Resolution established for the first time in history a 'corpus separatum' separating Jerusalem from the rest of the world and making it an international city governed by the United Nations.

The Resolution was rejected by the Arab nations, and so the city became divided into Israeli and Jordanian sectors. In an incredible fulfilment of Bible prophecy, May 1948 saw Israel being recognized as a nation once again after a gap of about two thousand years though the city remained divided until the Six Day War of 1967 when Israel finally took control of, and united, the city as the capital city of Israel.

This event was perhaps far more significant than many of us realize. Yes, it was a fulfilment of God's prophetic word. But this date in history marked the beginning of Zechariah's prophetic words:

Zechariah 12:10
I will pour out on the house of avid and the inhabitants of Jerusalem a spirit of compassion and supplication, so that, when they look on him whom they have pierced, they shall mourn for him, as on mourns for an only child, and weep bitterly over him, as one weeps over a first-born.

Just as Jesus had wept for His people and for Jerusalem, so a time is coming when the Jewish people will repent because they crucified their king. They will weep for Jesus just as He wept for them.

When this happens God will bring glory upon Zion. We will witness the fulfilment of Isaiah's words, who said:

Isaiah 60:1-3

Arise, shine, for your light has come, and the glory of the Lord has risen upon you. For behold darkness shall cover the earth, and thick darkness the peoples; but the Lord will arise upon you, and his glory will be seen upon you. All nations shall come to your light, and kings to the brightness of your rising.

As the darkness of evil comes upon the nations, the light of God will shine in Israel as a great number come to salvation. This is a nation where the end time signs will be most significantly revealed; the fig tree of Israel reveals the coming season.

On 7th June, 1967, General Moshe Dayan (1915-1981) spoke these words:[21]

This morning, the Israel Defence Forces liberated Jerusalem. We have united Jerusalem, the divided capital of Israel. We have returned to the holiest of our holy places, never to part from it again. To our Arab neighbours we extend, also at this hour – and with added emphasis at this hour – our hand in peace. And to our Christian and Muslim fellow citizens, we solemnly promise full religious freedom and rights. We did not come to Jerusalem for the sake of other peoples' holy places, and not to interfere with the adherents of other faiths, but in order to safeguard its entirety, and to live there together with others, in unity.

One of the important aspects of this unity is that Jerusalem is a city that accepts freedom of worship. It does not discriminate and it has guaranteed protection for holy sites.

Jerusalem is a place where fulfilment of many Old Testament prophecies has taken place. It is important because it is the place that God chose as His special 'dwelling' on earth. It is important because it is where Jesus as a child was 'offered' to God at the Temple. It is important because it was here that Jesus taught, where He was horribly crucified, and where He will return.

The remarkable story of Jerusalem is where unity of faith will be finally established. The Jewish people and the Gentiles will unite. It is where Jesus held the Last Supper and it is where the Holy Spirit came upon the disciples.

---

[21] *blog.standforisrael.org/articles/jerusalems-new-day-june-7-1967*

What we have learned from this brief review of Jerusalem and the Jewish people is that kingdoms have come and gone, rulers have come and gone, the Jewish people have suffered attacks and atrocities – and yet Jerusalem still stands, and the Jewish people are still united with their roots.

The small nation of Israel is less than three hundred miles long and nearly ninety miles wide at its widest point. It is prosperous and the world's eyes are upon it. This remarkable story of survival, often against great odds, can only be described as supernatural. It is a living testimony to God who has chosen this place and these people. Zechariah put these points into perspective in the words of this warning:

> Zechariah 2:8
> *For thus said the Lord of hosts, after his glory sent me to the nations who plundered you, for he who touches you touches the apple of his eye.*

This point leads us neatly into the next question and why it is so important to stand with and support Israel.

Why is praying for the peace of Jerusalem important?

The quick and simple answer to this question is encapsulated in the fact that as Jesus (Yeshua) came toward Jerusalem in His triumphal entry (soon to turn ugly) "he wept over it" (Luke 19:41). We too need to weep over Jerusalem. It was this city that God chose to be His special place and it was here that Jesus was crucified. It is Jerusalem where final peace will lay hold. When Jesus returns, the destruction of evil will give way to the peace and reign of God. We are called to pray for this peace – to eagerly usher in the return of Jesus and the peace of the kingdom.

Psalm 122 is a song of David for pilgrims going up to Jerusalem. It opens with the words, "I was glad when they said to me, 'Let us go to the House of the Lord!'" This is not only a song of gladness but also of gathering together and unity for it says, "Let us go," the destination being "the House of the Lord". The house of the Lord here refers to the Temple, which was utterly destroyed in 70AD and lies in ruins.

As we meditate on the words "I was glad" we might consider when the last time was that such joy and enthusiasm has filled our hearts at the thought of going to the house of God – to our local (or any other) church.

I am sorry to say that it has been a very long time for me. Why? Is it because I have lost my love and yearning to meet with God and His people? No! I hope that what I am about to say will not be considered uncharitable but there are many times when I have wondered what I am doing as I sit and listen to watered down messages, bands or groups of musicians leading worship with songs that are hard to join in, and extremely limited time in prayer; or shouts and dances ushering in the presence of the Holy Spirit, claiming His presence when in fact it is psychological hysteria or a blessing of the Spirit and not His presence. To all intent and purpose many of our churches, like the Temple in Jerusalem, lie in ruins.

There are many times when I have been spiritually moved to tears, even in churches and charismatic gatherings that we might consider our best. Not because of God's presence but because some try to manufacture it.

Now, I can hear many say, "But you have not been to our church..." That may be true; and praise God, because there are certainly pockets of Christian believers gathering together who keep God as the center of everything that is happening and give the Holy Spirit freedom to work. But they are far too few. It seems that generally we have become content with second best. If what we generally experience is the best then what happened to God's promises of the Holy Spirit and supernatural power?

I am not convinced that generally speaking we have really seen, or are seeing, manifestations of Pentecost, the Holy Spirit working in a way that we should experience in our churches and in our lives. We have the gifts but we do not have the power that goes with them. We have accepted second best instead of surrendering all with a hunger for the Holy Spirit and an expectancy that we will actually meet with God so that supernatural power will flow.

I cannot really express what I am talking about better than through the words of Smith Wigglesworth who in his inimitable and concise way said:[22]

> *I am positive that we are on the wrong side of the cross. We talk about love, love, love, but it ought to be repent, repent, repent. John the Baptist came, and his message was 'Repent', Jesus came with the same message: 'Repent'. The Holy Spirit came, and the message was the same: repent, repent, repent and believe. What has all this to do with Pentecost? Everything! It is the secret of our failure.*

The secret of our failure! I wonder how that has touched you; did you know that Jesus set a norm for our Christian living? The least that we should accept and expect was boldly summarized in these words:

John 14:12
Truly, truly, I say to you, he who believes in me will also do the works that I do; and greater works than these will he do, because I go to the father.

Did you notice those words, "he who believes in me"? This means that *all* who believe in Jesus are unmistakably included in this statement. If you believe in Jesus then you will do as He did.

What joy indeed there should actually be in the house of the Lord if we demonstrated the words of Jesus! The presence of God should tangibly be seen and felt. His Spirit should purely be present because, as the Psalmist said, "You are holy, who inhabit the praises of Israel" (Psalm 22:3, King James Version). All of this begins with repentance. If we do not truly repent and break down every barrier we will not see the supernatural in our lives.

If it were not for the Jewish people, those of us who are Gentiles would not enjoy what we have today. In Romans we read, "Through their trespass salvation has come to the Gentiles" (Romans 11:11). I am so grateful to those Jewish people who have repented of their wrongdoing and cried out to God. I am grateful to those Jewish people who have never given up honouring God. I am grateful that

---

[22] Taken from *Smith Wigglesworth Devotional* by Smith Wigglesworth. Copyright © (1999) by Whitaker House. Used by permission of Whitaker House. *www.whitakerhouse.com*

they firmly hold the vision that God's Temple will be re-built and His peace will return to Jerusalem. I am grateful to the increasing number of Jewish people today who are ascending the Mount in Jerusalem with gladness. I am grateful to those prophets such as Nehemiah and Daniel who repented over, and wept for, Jerusalem.

Nehemiah repented and with tears pleaded with God for Jerusalem, saying, "Lord, let thy ear be attentive to the prayer of thy servant, and to the prayer of thy servants who delight to fear thy name" (Nehemiah 1:11). Daniel also repented and mourned for his people and concluded by saying, "O Lord, hear; O Lord, forgive; O Lord, give heed and act; delay not, for thy own sake, O my God, because thy city and thy people are called by thy name" (Daniel 9:19). We too need to repent and not only pray to see God's supernatural hand in our churches but "pray for the peace of Jerusalem" (Psalm 122:6).

Let us now take a closer look at the original Hebrew translation of Psalm 122:6 in order to further our understanding as to why we need to pray for 'peace in Jerusalem'.

The Hebrew is *shaalu shalowm Yeruwshalaim shalah ahab*.

- *Shaalu* means 'ask, beg, enquire, salute or say hello'. People not going to Jerusalem would typically say this to the pilgrims.
- *Shalowm* means 'completeness in number, soundness in safety, peace with God and His covenant relationship.'
- *Yeruwshalaim* means 'teaching of double peace' and is the name given to Jerusalem in this text. It is worth noting that the spelling for Jerusalem is slightly different from that used earlier (Yerushalayim, meaning 'God sees or flows completeness, wholeness and peace'). The emphasis here is on the peace being expressed much as we might say today 'a double portion of peace'.
- *Shalah* means 'quiet' or 'at ease'
- *Ahab* means 'love'

The Jewish people are calling on God for the completeness and peace of Jerusalem. They are remembering these words:

Psalm 137:5,6

If I forget you, O Jerusalem, let my right hand wither! Let my tongue cleave to the roof of my mouth, if I do not remember you, if I do not set Jerusalem above my highest joy.

They are begging for Jerusalem to return to peace and ease with God through His presence in the Temple. They are begging to meet with Him in the Temple.

Paul quoted from Isaiah and said:

Romans 11:26,27

All Israel will be saved; as it is written, 'the deliverer will come from Zion, he will banish ungodliness from Jacob', 'and this will be my covenant with them when I take away their sins'.

When we pray for the peace of Jerusalem we are supporting the quest of the Jewish people and praying for our destiny, fulfilling our outreach responsibilities and hastening the return of Jesus because Israel must be restored and saved before Jesus returns.

When praying for Israel we should remember these words of Paul:

Romans 10:1-4

My heart's desire and prayer to God for them is that they may be saved. I bear them witness that they have a zeal for God, but it is not enlightened. For being ignorant of the righteousness that comes from God, and seeking to establish their own, they did not submit to God's righteousness. For Christ is the end of the law, that every one who has faith may be justified.

Let's hang our heads in shame over the fact that "they [the Jewish people] have a zeal for God" (Romans 10:2). Their understanding may not be enlightened but their zeal puts many of us to shame. Let us pray fervently for the mass salvation of the Jewish people and that our zeal will match theirs.

We owe an enormous debt of gratitude to the Jewish people because they have been faithful and meticulous guardians of the Word of God. God knew that like no other group of people on earth, the Jewish people would keep His word and stand firm and resolute with Him. Yes they have made mistakes but they always bounce back. God has always loved the Jewish people (see Deuteronomy 7:7,8) and He will keep His promises to them.

Isaiah wrote:

Isaiah 40:1,2
*Comfort, comfort my people, says your God. Speak tenderly to
Jerusalem, and cry to her that her warfare is ended, that her
iniquity is pardoned, that she has received from the Lord's hand
double for all her sins.*

It is important that we fully grasp what this scripture is saying;
therefore let's take a closer look at what Isaiah was proclaiming.

The Hebrew word used here for 'comfort' is *nacham* meaning 'to
regret, repent and console'. This is a consoling and comforting that
comes from an understanding heart – a heart of regret for lost
opportunities and sinfulness, and a heart of repentance. The word for
'warfare' is the Hebrew *tsaba* and means 'be in service and go out to
war'. What Isaiah is saying is that the time of fighting has ended. The
people have been forgiven. They have suffered twice (referring to the
destructions of the Temple), but now God is coming to take up His
rightful place. As Gentile Christians we have a responsibility to
appreciate, understand and comfort God's chosen people. We are to
stand with them and prepare the way for Christ to return through our
fervent prays for Jerusalem.

Elsewhere, talking about the restoration, honour and glory of
Israel, Isaiah speaks of a time when the prayers offered up for
Jerusalem will be answered. The Jewish people and their nation will
be able to rest, fearing nothing. If we needed an encouragement to
pray for Israel and for the peace of Jerusalem we find it in these
words:

Isaiah 62:6,7
*Upon your walls, O Jerusalem, I have set watchmen; all the day
and all the night they shall never be silent. You who put the Lord
in remembrance, take no rest, and give him no rest until he
establishes Jerusalem and makes it a praise in the earth.*

Three times a day the Jewish people pray a prayer that has been
faithfully repeated for about two thousand years: "May it be your
will that the Temple be speedily rebuilt in our own time." We are
living in a time that sits at the brink of seeing this prayer answered
and prophecy fulfilled.

Rebuilding of the third Temple

This issue is extremely complex and would really take a book of its own to explain and do justice to the historical, political and religious debate.

Currently, the Temple Mount has become a political issue. The mount is under Muslim administrative control, and no non-Muslim excavation, exploration or prayer is permitted on it. Both Jewish and Gentile people are considered 'unclean', though the ruling Muslim Waqf[23] does allow limited and controlled tourist visits.

Jewish people, particularly Orthodox Jewish people, have been praying for the restoration of the Temple since its demise in 70AD. The Old Testament prophet Amos concludes his writings with these prophetic words about God's end time kingdom blessings for His chosen people:

Amos 9:14,15
I will restore the fortunes of my people Israel, and they shall rebuild the ruined cities and inhabit them; they shall plant vineyards and drink their wine, and they shall make gardens and eat their fruit. I will plant them upon their land, and they shall never again be plucked up out of the land which I have given them.

Bible prophecies about the last days say that the Jewish people will return from exile to their homeland. As we have already seen, the astounding fulfilment of this prophecy took place sixty-five years ago in May 1948. Added to this prophecy Amos said something that the world should take note of. I am of course referring to God's promise, "They shall never again be plucked up out of the land which I have given them." (Amos 9: 15).

Amos also said that the cities would be rebuilt and prosperity in the land will flow. Rebuilding the ruins includes the Temple. Just sixty-five years after the Jewish people returned to their promised land Israel is flourishing and effectively self-sufficient. Preparations for the rebuilding of the Temple are complete.

The Six Day War of 1967 was in many ways a mirror or a sort of rehearsal for the battle of Gog and Magog, which we will talk more

---

[23] *waqf* means 'confinement and prohibition' or 'to stop, detain and keep still'

about in the next chapter. It was nothing short of miraculous that Israel without help from its allies overcame great odds and emerged victorious. Following this remarkable victory, General Moshe Dayan and his troops not only quadrupled its land but notably brought Jerusalem under Israeli control. Fittingly Moshe Dayan placed a note in the Western Wall, which quoting from Psalm 118:23 simply says, "This is the Lord's doing; it is marvelous in our eyes."

From 1970, plans to re-build the Temple in Jerusalem have found new impetus. During the course of this time about 500,000 Jewish people have come to Jesus.

In late 2004 the ancient Sanhedrin Council of Rabbis suddenly reconvened in Tiberias, the place where they had last met sixteen hundred years ago. This significant re-establishment of the Sanhedrin Council is important because they are widely seen as the overseers of the third Temple construction, and indeed, in mid 2005 it was publicly declared by them that they would re-build the Temple.

The Israeli Temple Institute has already completed an operational blueprint to build the Temple. They have also piece by piece started to rebuild the required working and ceremonial aspects of this temple and it is, as we speak, taking shape. Levite priests have already been fully trained, and they are waiting to serve in the Temple. Another group, the Temple Mount Faithful, have even cut stones for the Temple structure.

What we are witnessing is a divine coming together of end time prophesies. Everything is in place for a speedy re-building of the Temple.

The Jewish people take very seriously these words:

Exodus 25:8
Make me a sanctuary, that I may dwell in their midst.

The situation may seem impossible for this event to take place. But although we do not know how or exactly when God's word will be finally accomplished we can rest assured that it will come to pass.

2 Corinthians 6:1,2
Working together with him, then, we entreat you not to accept the grace of God in vain. For he says, 'At the acceptable time I have listened to you, and helped you on the day of salvation'. Behold, now is the acceptable time; behold, now is the day of salvation.

CHAPTER FOUR

Gog of Magog

Ezekiel 38:18,19
When Gog shall come against the land of Israel, says the Lord God,: my wrath will be roused. For in my jealousy and in my blazing wrath I declare, on that day there shall be a great shaking in the land of Israel.

Seed thought

God is about to take His church into a wilderness of testing, to strip away our human resources and make us wholly dependent on Him and to bring us into His rest! Tragically, God's rest remains largely unclaimed by His people today. Rest is total trust in God for all things. How do we prepare for the storm? Our place of safety is our secret closet of prayer! The darker things get, the brighter our Lord's light will shine.

- David Wilkerson[24]

Introduction

Well over two and a half thousand years ago Ezekiel proclaimed an important 'last days' prophecy. The prophecy is specific and detailed in many ways apart from the exact timing and chronology of some of the related events. It tells us that in the last days there will be a ferocious attack on Israel with a view to wiping the nation out. A conjoining of forces from several nations surrounding its borders and

---

[24] *God's Plan to Protect His People in the Coming Depression*, 1998, Wilkerson Trust Publications

their coalition will carry out this attack even though a peace covenant is in place at the time.

There is much debate about exactly which nations will ally against Israel. I would not claim expert status, and so much of this may best be left to the scholars though for our purposes here consensus seems to include Arab nations, Turkey, Russia (or at least its weaponry) and Islamic republics of Central Asia. Having said this Ezekiel adds:

Ezekiel 3:13
Sheba and Dedan and the merchants of Tarshish and all its villages will say to you, 'Have you come to seize spoil? Have you assembled your hosts to carry off plunder, to carry away silver and gold, to take away cattle and goods, to seize great spoil?'

Because this scripture suggests that Sheba and Dedan are questioning the motives of the aggressor, it seems that some Arab or Islamic nations, possibly from the Arabian Peninsular, or Ethiopia and Yemen along with the merchants of Western Europe nations and their allies, will only watch and not be part of the Gog invasion.

For various reasons, including geographical changes over time, the nomadic nature of these groups and different references that seem to speak about dissimilar groups, it is not easy to pinpoint exactly what or whom Ezekiel is actually referring to.

As I have indicated, because of the complexity and changing geographical map there have been many interpretations and claims made. These even suggest that parts of the old Roman Empire (Italy) and Greece (Greco-Macedonian Empire) will be among the Gog invasion. Many of these exponents, although persuasive in arguments and presentations, often mix modern-day countries with Bible-day empires, countries or regions, many of which of course do not exist today. It is for these reasons that I apply a degree of caution.

The fascinating inclusion of Arabia as possible non-aggressors may make some sense as, unlike the other Arab countries, these are not historically descendants of Ishmael. What is more certain is the fact that there will be a very large invasion force of several nations that according to Ezekiel's prophecy will attack the 'small' nation of Israel and surround it. For our purposes it is best to consider the arguments but primarily watch the signs.

Ezekiel graphically describes what Gog and his allies will do to Israel in these words:

Ezekiel 38:8,9

After many days you will be mustered; in the latter years you will go against the land that is restored from war, the land where people were gathered from many nations upon the mountains of Israel, which had been a continual waste; its people were brought out from the nations and now dwell securely, all of them. You will advance, coming on like a storm; you will be like a cloud covering the land, you and all your hordes, and many peoples with you.

As we read further we discover that the invading force intention is to "seize spoil and carry off plunder; to assail the waste places which are now inhabited'" (Ezekiel 38:12). In other words the intention is to overrun and destroy Israel.

It is worth adding at this juncture another interesting reference in scripture that refers to Israel's aggressors. I refer here to Psalm 83 and the encirclement of Israel.

Psalm 83

There are extensive disagreements among scholars about Psalm 83. Some claim that it is a prophecy that has already taken place whilst others claim that it is something that will happen before the Ezekiel prophecy. Still others believe Psalm 83 is part of the Gog and Magog prophecy. With this in mind readers should please be aware that in placing this piece within the context of the Gog and Magog chapter it does not mean that I agree with this last point or with any others mentioned here.[25]

Turning our thoughts back to Psalm 83 we find a list of protagonists mentioned:

Psalm 83:6-8

...the tents of Edom and the Ishmaelites, Moab and the Hagrites, Gebal and Ammon and Amalek, Philistia with the inhabitants of Tyre; Assyria also has joined them; they are the strong arm of the children of Lot.

---

[25] See Appendix III

Let's take a closer look at this list, some of who were originally relatives of Israel:

- *Edom:* The descendants of Jacob's brother Esau, now modern-day Jordan.
- *Ishmaelites:* Descended from Ishmael, now located somewhere south of Saudi Arabia.
- *Moab:* This now falls within modern-day Jordan.
- *Hagrites:* Today this area points to Egypt.
- *Gebal:* Modern-day Lebanon.
- *Ammon:* This is another group that now falls within the boundaries of modern-day Jordan.
- *Amalek:* A region now south of Israel occupied by modern-day Palestinians.
- *Philistia:* An area known today as Gaza.
- *Tyre:* Today known as Lebanon.
- *Assyria:* Now on the border of Syria and in modern-day Iraq.

The enemies of Israel cited in Psalm 83 have not all been at enmity with her at the same time. Some believe that this is evidence to show that this event has not yet taken place because it refers to all the groups mentioned in one single attack as suggested in verse five, which says, "They conspire with one accord; against thee they make a covenant". The differences between this scripture and Ezekiel's prophecy also suggest different timings. But it is important to understand that we have no definitive answers to support many of the claims made by some scholars.

As we investigate the arguments it is noticeable that many writers place emphasis on recent and current conflicts or possible future conflicts and political situations, some of which 'colour' the conclusions reached. Few actually point to firm scripture support for what they are saying. I am not trying to introduce provocation, but in this sense they leave us with an academic argument with little or no Bible support. These academic arguments may prove helpful in placing some of the jigsaw together, but let's keep our primary focus on what we can positively glean from scripture and not on speculation.

It is tragic that Christian believers fall out over who is right and who is wrong on issues that have little overall spiritual importance.

Where we do not have definitive answers we should apply integrity and honestly declare it.

The context of this Psalm is a prayer to God asking for Him to judge those who bring enmity and aggression upon Israel. The Psalm talks about Israel being circled by her enemies who in their ungodly hearts purpose to obliterate her. The prayer seeks not only that God will protect Israel but also it concludes with these words:

Psalm 83:17,18
Let them be put to shame and dismayed forever; let them perish in disgrace. Let them know that thou alone, whose name is the Lord, art the Most High over all the earth.

Here the prayer goes beyond simply seeking the overthrow of Israel's enemies. An even greater purpose is faithfully sought that goes beyond personal survival. The Psalm concludes by asking that God will eventually be glorified in such a way that these aggressors will acknowledge Him as the Most High and turn to Him.

What we have being played out in graphical and demonstrable witness is the battle between the kingdoms of darkness and of Heaven. It is the physical demonstration of a spiritual conflict first mentioned in Genesis:

Genesis 3:15
I will put enmity between you and the woman, and between your seed and her seed; he shall bruise your head, and you shall bruise his heel.

Satan is at war with God and His people as he attempts to overthrow and destroy anything to do with God. Though the odds may seem impossible the result will be God's victory and triumph. God will gather His faithful to Himself.

Psalm 83 is an outward expression of faith, love and forgiveness in the face of adversity. In a similar way Jesus said:

Matthew 5:44,45
I say to you, Love your enemies and pray for those who persecute you, so that you may be sons of your father who is in heaven; for he makes his sun rise on the evil and on the good, and sends rain on the just and the unjust.

In chapter two we discussed the strategic importance of God's end time plan that led to the amazing fulfilment of Ezekiel's prophecy in chapters 36 and 37. By way of reminder, these stated that Israel would become a nation once again. The year 1948 saw this seemingly impossible prophecy remarkably come to fruition. This fulfilment now paves the way for Ezekiel's prophetic words in the next chapters thirty-eight and thirty-nine – a prophecy that could not be fulfilled unless Israel had become a thriving and prosperous nation!

Ezekiel repeats over and again in his prophecies that God will prove Himself to the world. This is also the case in and through the attack led by Gog upon Israel:

> **Ezekiel 38:21-23**
> *I will summon every kind of terror against Gog, says the Lord God; every man's sword will be against his brother [it appears here that the allies will turn on one another]. With pestilence and bloodshed I will enter into judgment with him; and I will rain upon him, torrential rains and hailstorms, fire and brimstone. So I will show my greatness and my holiness and make myself known in the eyes of many nations. Then they will know that I am the Lord.*

This will be a terrible, awesome time. The land of Israel will shake violently, and we read that these events will affect the entire world.

> **Ezekiel 38:20**
> *All the men that are upon the face of the earth, shall quake at my presence, and the mountains shall be thrown down, and the cliffs shall fall, and every wall shall tumble to the ground.*

Although time, dates and circumstances are in God's hands and not specifically revealed, the signs are clearly highlighted for us. As our eyes fix upon the small nation of Israel it is becoming increasingly clear that the likelihood of Ezekiel's prophetic message being fulfilled in our lifetime is a growing and fast approaching reality.

It is not entirely clear at what stage the events of the Rapture and tribulation will take place, but being primed and ready is most certainly a matter of urgency. It is for this reason that this chapter is vitally included as a basis for prayer and seeking God in a way perhaps not done by many of us before.

The urgency placed upon my heart is that there really is no time for procrastination. We surely do not want to suddenly be caught doing anything other than being immersed in God's will for our lives. But, of course you may reasonably ask some personal questions such as "What am I looking for?" "What is going to happen?" These are good questions that show a keen spirit. They are questions that this chapter will seek to cover along with a few others.

Gog of Magog

Ezekiel stated that the word of the Lord had come to him saying:

Ezekiel 38:1,2
Son of man, set your face toward Gog, of the land of Magog, the chief prince of Meshech and Tubal and prophesy against him.

This clearly states that there is a person, not literally called Gog but a person with recognition as the chief prince or leader, a political and military leader of the land of Magog.

The names Magog, Meshech and Tubal feature in the Old Testament book of Genesis where we learn that Japheth, the son of Noah had seven sons – Magog, Meshech and Tubal being three of these who are historically associated with the Goths, Cretans, Scythians and Russians. Interestingly some writers include Russia and even Rome, both of which have also been implicated by some dispensational writers.[26] But as already stated we must consider the biblical map of the day and the terminology used by the Bible writers. The areas that these and other prophecies point to are Turkey and the Islamic states near or surrounding Israel. Why do I say this? Let's take a look at a few scriptures:

Zechariah 9:13
For I have bent Judah as my bow; I have made Ephraim its arrow. I will banish your sons, O Zion, over your sons, O Greece, and wield you like a warrior's sword.

The reference to Greece in this scripture is ancient Greece and its empire – and actually refers to what is now modern-day Turkey. Syria was also originally part of the ancient Greek Empire.

Isaiah 10:34
He will cut down the thickets of the forest with an axe, and Lebanon with its majestic trees will fall.

Lebanon is clearly warned about God's wrath.

---

[26] See Appendix I

Isaiah 19:1
An oracle concerning Egypt. Behold, the Lord is riding on a swift cloud and comes to Egypt; and the idols of Egypt will tremble at his presence, and the heart of the Egyptians will melt within them.

Again, we see Egypt coming under God's wrath.

What we do know is that Ezekiel says that Gog will descend "from your place out of the uttermost parts of the north, you and many peoples with you" (Ezekiel 38:15). We are also told that the army rising against Israel will come from "Persia [now called Iran], Cush (Kush) [this area is not known for certain, possibly south of Egypt, Sudan and Somalia], and Put [now Libya]" (Ezekiel 38:5) and "Gomer and all his hordes; Bethtogarmah [areas somewhere north of the Black sea] from the uttermost parts of the north with all his hordes" (Ezekiel 38:5,6).

Although there is a lack of detail, Jesus reveals a very interesting end time fact for us in these words:

Revelation 2:12,13 (KJV)
And to the angel of the church in Pergamos [Pergamum] write, "These things says He who has the sharp two-edged sword: 'I know your works, and where you dwell, where Satan's throne is. And you hold fast to My name, and did not deny my faith even in the days in which Antipas was My faithful martyr, who was killed among you, where Satan dwells.'"

Pergamon was part of the ancient Greek Empire and, it seems, now found in modern-day Aeolis, near the Aegean Sea in Turkey.

Chrislam

Yes – that is what I thought when I first came across this word: what is it? Beneath our noses a new religious sect was born in the 1980's. As the name suggests it is a mix of both Christianity and Islam. Two opposite beliefs about the Trinity and deity of Jesus Christ have conjoined!

The subtlety is that Chrislam is known as 'The Will of God Mission', 'The True Message of God Mission' or 'The Mountain of Loosing Bondage (God's Love) Mission'. This new religion is growing fast, spreading throughout the world, including America where many have embraced it. Advocates of this religion see it as a solution to conflicts between Christian and Muslim.

There are many advocates who say that the Church must adapt to society, and indeed in one way or another churches have done this in various ways and from one extreme to another. The Church has never been guided in scripture to adapt to society. We must not confuse loving one another and our neighbour with compromising and adapting our faith. What we are seeing is a falling away from the faith as churches, ministers and Christians alike embrace modern society. No longer is Jesus the head of the Church and the Bible its guide and training resource.

In his first letter John said:

> 1 John 4:2,3
> *Every spirit that confesses that Jesus Christ has come in the flesh is of God, and every spirit that does not confess Jesus is not of God. This is the spirit of antichrist, of which you have heard that it is coming, and now it is in the world already.*

Many have thought that the Antichrist is purely someone or something that will reveal himself or something will happen in the future, just before Jesus returns. This scripture however tells us that the spirit of antichrist is already with us.

Who or what is the Antichrist?

The meaning of the term 'antichrist' is actually explained in the word itself. The prefix 'anti' means 'to oppose, be against or instead of' Christ. The antichrist may come in *direct opposition* or, more likely, in *subtle opposition* to Christ. The word 'antichrist' is uniquely mentioned in both letters of John (1 John 2:18-22; 4:3 and 2 John :7), who is the only person to use this particular word in the New Testament. It was however a term or concept that was not unknown in Judaism. Jesus himself, though not using the word, did warn His disciples about false Christs (Matthew 24:5,23,24 and Mark 13:21,22), and Paul spoke of "the man of lawlessness [or sin]" (2 Thessalonians 2:3).

What we can conclude from these scriptures is that there is a significant difference between false Christs, meaning those who have claimed the status of Christ, and the end time Antichrist who might be far more cunning and subtle by not overtly denying Christ and

God; the Antichrist may be far more difficult to detect than we might expect. The spirit of the antichrist has already deceived many, notably those that have embraced such cults as Chrislam, humanism, secularism and New Age philosophies, to name but a few.

The 'name of the game' is deception. We must jealously guard against spiritual deception. In his book 'Man, The Dwelling Place of God', Aiden Wilson Tozer (1897-1963) includes a section called 'How to try the spirits' where he says:[27]

> *Strange as it may seem, the danger today is greater for the fervent Christian than for the lukewarm and the self-satisfied. The seeker after God's best things is eager to hear anyone who offers a way by which he can obtain them. He longs for some new experience, some elevated view of truth, some operation of the Spirit that will raise him above the dead level of religious mediocrity he sees all around him, and for this reason he is ready to give a sympathetic ear to the new and the wonderful in religion, particularly if it is presented by someone with an attractive personality and a reputation for superior godliness.*

These words are perhaps more important for us today than they have ever been.

If we do not keep our gaze firmly on Jesus and check all things against scripture we leave ourselves open to deception. Our hunger and thirst must take us to God. Watered down preaching and teaching in our churches leaves us vulnerable and open to deception. The Holy Spirit is our teacher and counsellor. We need him more than ever before. Spiritual deception is rife.

We do not have precise details of the Antichrist other than that he will be a powerful, astute and cunning leader who will come in the guise of peace and prosperity. There are two particularly revealing scriptures that are noteworthy:

Daniel 8:25
By his cunning he shall make deceit prosper under his hand, and in his own mind he shall magnify himself. Without warning he shall destroy many; and he shall even rise up against the Prince of princes; but, by no human hand, he shall be broken.

---

[27] *Man. The Dwelling Place of God.* Compiled by Anita M Bailey 1966, Christian Publications

1 Thessalonians 5:3
When people say, 'There is peace and security,' then sudden destruction will come upon them as travail comes upon a woman with child, and there will be no escape.

As Christians we have been clearly warned about these things; Jesus will come and break the Antichrist.

The attack and defeat of Gog

In Ezekiel 38 and 39 and Revelation 20 we read that there will be a terrible, evil attack on God's chosen people and His land Israel.

This invasion of Israel is often referred to as the war of Gog and Magog. I have referred to Gog *of* Magog based upon the fact that Ezekiel states very clearly that Gog refers to the leader of the invasion on Israel who comes from Magog. We often however also read about Gog *and* Magog. I have simply identified that this relates to the leader, his country and the allied armies under Gog.

We know from the scriptures that the invasion on Israel will be vicious. It will also be a war that will invoke the wrath of God and a supernatural victory that will be so dramatic that the world will notice who is behind it. Ezekiel declares this God inspired message:

Ezekiel 38:23
So I will show my greatness and my holiness and make myself known in the eyes of many nations. Then they will know that I am the Lord.

God will openly reveal His power

Yes, God Himself will dramatically intervene in the overwhelming invasion of Israel, and, as previously noted, Ezekiel tells us that God will "rain upon him and his hordes and the many peoples that are with him, torrential rains and hailstorms, fire and brimstone" (Ezekiel 38:22) from heaven. It will destroy so many of the attackers of Israel that it will take seven months to bury the dead.

How do I know this? Let's take a look at what Ezekiel prophesied:

Ezekiel 39:5,6
You [this refers to the invading forces led by Gog] shall fall in the open field; for I have spoken, says the Lord God. I will send

fire on Magog and on those who dwell securely in the
coastlands; and they shall know that I am the Lord.

It appears from this verse that God will not only vindicate His
name against Gog and the invading forces on the battlefield but He
will also destroy the homeland of Gog: Magog. And as we read a few
verses further on we find these words:

Ezekiel 39:11,12
On that day I will give to Gog a place for burial in Israel, the
Valley of the Travelers east of the sea; it will block the travelers,
for there and all his multitude will be buried; it will be called the
Valley of Hamon-gog. For seven months the house of Israel will
be burying them, in order to cleanse the land.

Ezekiel paints for us a terrible picture of slaughter upon those
who come against God's land and His people. But when in the overall
end time plans of God will this happen?

God's end time plan

As already stated, Bible scholars disagree about the definite order
of the timeline of events in the last days. For example, Ezekiel has
clearly prophesied the attack upon Israel by Gog of Magog, but
whether this will take place before the Rapture, alongside it or after is
not made totally clear.

I neither presume to argue with Bible scholars nor wish to engage
in arguments. It is very easy to get caught up in academic argument,
disagreement and misunderstanding about these things and to lose
sight of the important issues; or to take the opposite stance – do
nothing and say, "What will happen will happen." Neither of these
positions is healthy or correct.

The Old Testament prophet Isaiah said:

Isaiah 28:9,10
Whom will he teach knowledge, and to whom will he explain the
message? Those who are weaned from the milk, those taken
from the breast? For it is precept upon precept, precept upon
precept, line upon line, line upon line, here a little, there a little.

Effectively this is an explanation of the fact that God's messages
to us are both scattered throughout scripture and are there for us to
find, read, study and pray over. They act, among many other things,

as warnings and indicators with the purpose of keeping us alert and ready. This point is further illustrated for us in Revelation chapter three where we read:

> **Revelation 3:2,3**
> *Awake, and strengthen what remains and is on the point of death, for I have not found your works perfect in the sight of my God. Remember then what you received and heard; keep that, and repent. If you will not awake, I will come like a thief, and you will not know at what hour I will come upon you.*

Sitting back and doing nothing is not an option. Jesus warned against this in the parable of the ten maidens. We should also not spend our time and focus on arguments, disagreements and predictions but rather read God's word, seek Him face to face and above all watch and be fully prepared and ready. This theme – watch and be ready – is earnestly repeated many times, and so clearly this is exactly what we should do.

Please do not misunderstand. I am not saying that it is wrong to see if there are answers or clues that we should be aware of in scripture. I am saying that we must take care over where we place our focus and energy. If our focus moves us away from setting our eyes on the Lord and remaining in constant readiness then it may signify that the time has come to reconsider our situation. We must also guard against falling into fruitless and pointless disagreements and arguments, especially those that lead to division, pride and even bitterness.

The Bible says that we must ready ourselves in repentance, humility, forgiveness, spreading the gospel and living in God's supernatural power. It is about our light shining brightly with plenty in reserve because the Holy Spirit is upon us. I for one do not want my spiritual walk found like the five foolish maidens whose lights were flickering and with no oil reserves.

The Christian believer has a calling to spread the gospel message. As prophecy unravels we can show people who God is. Everything around us may seem to fall apart, and the situation may look hopeless; but by the cross of Jesus there is hope, salvation and victory. Time is however running out. Jesus may return at any time.

The Rapture

As we consider the imminent return of Jesus this naturally leads us to think about what has become known as the Rapture or the snatching away of the Church. The Church in this context does not mean 'church' as we generally refer to it today such as a denomination or congregation. It means the true believers of Christ who will be suddenly taken to join him in the air on their way to the kingdom of heaven.

Put simply, the Rapture refers to the time when the dead in Christ resurrect and those true believers who are alive at the time of Christ's return will rise up into heaven. This is all explained for us in the following two scriptures:

> 1 Corinthians 15:51,52
> *Lo! I tell you a mystery. We shall not all sleep, but we shall all be changed, in a moment, in the twinkling of an eye, at the last trumpet. For the trumpet will sound, and the dead will be raised imperishable, and we shall be changed.*

> 1 Thessalonians 4:15-18
> *For this we declare to you by the word of the Lord, that we who are alive, who are left until the coming of the Lord, shall not precede those who have fallen asleep. For the Lord himself will descend from heaven with a cry of command, with the archangel's call, and with the sound of the trumpet of God. And the dead in Christ will rise first; then we who are alive, who are left, shall be caught up together with them in the clouds to meet the Lord in the air; and so we shall always be with the Lord. Therefore comfort one another with these words.*

We are naturally inquisitive, and so many ask, "When will this happen?" Anyone asking this question is in good company. The disciples of Jesus said, "Tell us, when will this be, and what will be the sign of your coming and the close of the age?'" (Matthew 24:3). Some today go even further and ask if this event will take place pre-tribulation, mid-tribulation or post-tribulation.

As an aside, the theories concerning the timing of the Rapture are presented later in this chapter. But I confess at this juncture that I do not pretend to know the answer. As far as I am able to establish the Bible is not absolutely clear about this question other than to say that only God knows the time and date.

What we do know is the very first response of Jesus to His disciples' question is actually a re-occurring message: "Take heed that no one leads you astray" (Matthew 24:4). Jesus goes on to warn that some will claim that they are the Christ, there will be rumours, and there will be disasters, tribulation and hatred. Many will fall away. False prophets will arise, and many people will grow hard and cold toward God. Wickedness toward one another will increase. But, keep going in faith and belief. Keep spreading the gospel message and then the end will come.

Paul warns against trying to set a timetable and whilst writing to the Thessalonians he says:

1 Thessalonians 5:1,2
As to the times and the seasons, brethren, you have no need to have anything written to you. For you yourselves know well that the day of the Lord will come like a thief in the night.

Paul does not leave it there, however; he goes on to say:

1 Thessalonians 5:8
Since we belong to the day, let us be sober, and put on the breastplate of faith and love, and for a helmet the hope of salvation.

You see, Paul, like Jesus, was more concerned about making sure that people maintained their faith in God. They should remain fully alert and ready and not enter into speculation or suggest that it is possible to predict a specific time within which Christ will return.

Having said this, Jesus did leave a clue for us and the Jewish people. He said to His disciples:

Matthew 24:15-21
When you see the desolating sacrilege spoken of by the prophet Daniel, standing in the holy place (let the reader understand), then let those who are in Judea flee to the mountains; let him who is on the housetop not go down to take what is in his house, and let him who is in the field not turn back to take his mantle. And alas for those who are with child and for those who give suck in these days! Pray that your flight may not be in winter or on a Sabbath. For then there will be great tribulation, such as has not been from the beginning of the world until now, no, and never will be.

Jesus specifically points to Daniel's prophecy, and so this would be a good place to go and find out what's made known for us in these words. But before we consider this Jesus went on to speak a little about His return and He said:

> **Matthew 24:29-31**
> *Immediately after the tribulation of those days the sun will be darkened, and the moon will not give its light, and the stars will fall from heaven, and the powers of the heavens will be shaken; then will appear the sign of the Son of man in heaven, and then all the tribes of the earth will mourn, and they will see the Son of man coming on the clouds of heaven with power and great glory; and he will send out his angels with a loud trumpet call, and they will gather his elect from the four winds, from one end of heaven to the other.*

This outline of Christ's return states very clearly that these events will occur "immediately after the tribulation". Some argue that what is not crystal clear is the reference "all the tribes of the earth" and "his elect". Do these refer to the twelve Jewish tribes and the chosen, the 144,000, or does it include the Church? A search of the original translation suggests that this refers to every believer.[28]

It is partly for these reasons that differing views are held about the sequence of events. In order to understand these views a little better let's take a very brief overview of the points that each make.

Pre-tribulation Rapture argument

This is probably the most widely accepted view among scholars. Daniel's 70th week prophecy suggests that the church of true believers will suddenly be taken to dwell with Jesus in safety whilst those left will suffer the seven years of the great tribulation. During the course of these seven years the Jewish people will recognize Jesus as the promised Messiah and be saved. Those remaining will finally be judged at the coming of Christ.

This argument would make sense of the frequent warnings that the Bible gives about not knowing the time or season when Jesus will

---

[28] Useful web sites for original Greek text and word meaning search can be found in the bibliography

call His believers. If this event were to take place after the start of the tribulation there would be a clear sign of it coming seven years later.

Mid-tribulation Rapture argument

Those holding this view number the smallest group of scholars. They suggest that midway through Daniel's seven years, at the three-and-a-half-year point, before God pours out His wrath, the Rapture will take place. This argument is generally used because tribulation is something that we are specifically told will happen and the church will be party to it.

Another argument that is sometimes used in support of this view comes from the words of Paul who said:

2 Thessalonians 2:3,4
Let no one deceive you in any way; for that day will not come, unless the rebellion comes first, and the man of lawlessness is revealed, the son of perdition, who opposes and exalts himself against every so-called god or object of worship, so that he takes his seat in the temple of God, proclaiming himself to be God.

Also, Paul goes on to say:

2 Thessalonians 2:8
The lawless one will be revealed, and the Lord Jesus will slay him with the breath of his mouth and destroy him by his appearing and his coming.

Paul states clearly here that the "day will not come, unless the rebellion comes first, and the man of lawlessness is revealed". It appears that four things will take place before Jesus returns:

- There will be a falling away or rebellion.
- The man of lawlessness or sin will be revealed.
- The man of sin will exalt himself above God.
- The man of sin will seat himself in the temple of God.

The announcement of a seven-year covenant described in Daniel 9:27 is a key sign for believers to watch out for.

Post-tribulation Rapture argument

The belief here is that the true believers, the church, will go through the entire tribulation period. Those holding this view also believe that the parable of the wheat and tares indicates that a separation of the saved and the unsaved will occur at the end of the age, taking these words as their evidence:

> **Matthew 13:30**
> *Let both grow together until the harvest; and at the harvest time*
> *I will tell the reapers, gather the weeds first and bind them in*
> *bundles to be burned, but gather the wheat into my barn.*

As we can see from these differing views, knowing the time when Jesus will come appears 'fuzzy'. Our Jewish friends celebrate different feasts throughout the year. We will take a look at these in chapter five; however it is useful for us to understand that these feasts both help the Jews and help us to see what God has done and what He is going to do. The birth, life and death of Jesus have, as we will discover in more detail later, fulfilled the springtime or early rain feasts of Passover, Unleavened Bread, First Fruits and Pentecost. The autumn or latter rain feasts have not yet been fully fulfilled. These are the feast of Trumpets, Atonement and Tabernacles.

The reason for mentioning these feasts at this time is because Messianic Jewish believers understand that the feast of Trumpets is a forerunner of the Rapture. It is on this day that the Jewish people blow their trumpets (*shofar*). Paul said:

> **1 Corinthians 15:51,52**
> *We shall not all sleep [not all will die], but we shall all be*
> *changed, in a moment, in the twinkling of an eye, at the last*
> *trumpet. For the trumpet will sound, and the dead will be raised*
> *imperishable, and we shall be changed.*

It is widely believed that this event will trigger the seven-year tribulation. This therefore supports the Pre-tribulation view.

The feast of Trumpets is interesting because although it takes place in September / October the precise day of its beginnings is unknown. It is a day requiring verification by two witnesses who confirm a new moon and blow a trumpet to herald its start. The particular relevance of this point fits with something that we read in Revelation 11:3, which says:

> *And I will grant my two witnesses power to prophesy for one*
> *thousand two hundred and sixty days, clothed in sackcloth.*

The 1260 days equate to 42 months or 3½ years. The timings fit with the prophecy of Daniel, and so we will look at this shortly.

This means that whatever view we personally hold, it is extremely wise to ready ourselves for the Rapture to happen at any time. Having said this, we do have some further clues to consider.

Paul writes in his second letter to the church in Thessalonica about the question that we too ask, namely when Jesus will return, and he said:

2 Thessalonians 2:3,4

Let no one deceive you in any way; for that day [verse one explains what 'that day' refers to and explains that it is the coming of our Lord Jesus Christ], will not come, unless the rebellion comes first, and the man of lawlessness is revealed, the son of perdition, who opposes and exalts himself against every so-called god or object of worship, so that he takes his seat in the temple of God, proclaiming himself to be God.

This scripture is important so let's take a closer look at what it really means.

Verse three first tells us that the coming of Jesus "will not come, unless" two things happen first:

- *The rebellion comes first.*
  The Greek word used here for rebellion is *apostasia* meaning 'to fall away, forsake or defect'.
- *The man of lawlessness is revealed.*
  The Greek word used here is *anomia* meaning 'having contempt for the law and righteousness, violating these, a man of sin'. He is also called the son of perdition. The Greek word for perdition used here is *apoleia* meaning 'the son of destruction and ruin'.

The rebellion talked about here refers to apostasy, many falling away from the faith and their first love. We are already seeing this happening, and it will increase as we see people being sucked into a different gospel message and the continuing watering down of the scriptures in our churches.

Christians argue publicly with one another about scripture, bringing forward their own interpretations and ideas. It is not about what we think; it is about what the Bible says. We must carefully scrutinize the scriptures, test them and come before God.

Whatever view we may take about the second coming of Christ, the tribulation and Rapture, there is one message: Jesus is coming back, the age is coming to an end and we must watch and be ready. None of us know when Jesus will return!

Daniel's prophecy and the close of the age

We have briefly talked about the tribulation, but what is it? The tribulation is a seven-year period when Israel will take centre stage in the world, many Jewish people will realize who exactly Jesus is and God will judge nations. This time will be so bad that Jesus says, "If those days had not been shortened, no human being would be saved; but for the sake of the elect those will be shortened" (Matthew 24:22).

According to Daniel's prophecy this period will begin with a peace agreement between Israel and a number of other nations. At some stage during this period it seems that the Temple will be rebuilt.

Daniel's prophecy comes amidst an open confession of sin and repentance because Israel had not kept God's commands and instead acted wickedly. Daniel prayed fervently for forgiveness and asked:

> Daniel 9:17,18
> *O our God, hearken to the prayer of thy servant and to his supplications, and for thy own sake, O Lord, cause thy face to shine upon thy sanctuary, which is desolate. O my God, incline your ear and hear; open thy eyes and behold our desolations, and the city which is called by thy name; for we do not present our supplications before thee on the ground of our righteousness, but on the ground of thy great mercy.*

Daniel not only sought forgiveness for Israel but he claimed the promises that God had given for His people and land, throwing himself and the people of Israel on the mercy of God.

Daniel's prayer instigated the sudden appearance of the angel Gabriel who said:

> Daniel 9:24
> *Seventy weeks of years are decreed concerning your people and you holy city, to finish the transgression, to put an end to sin,*

and to atone for iniquity, to bring an everlasting righteousness, to seal both vision and prophet, and to anoint a most holy place.

Arising from Daniel's repentance and promise-claiming prayer, God's grace and mercy put in place a timeframe to get right with God.

The timeframe given to Daniel is seventy weeks of years. Most scholars agree that the interpretation of "weeks of years" is that each day of the week counts as one year and so each week covers a seven-year span. This means that the "seventy weeks" is 70 x 7 = 490 years in total.[29]

As we read further we discover that the four hundred and ninety weeks are subdivided into three different time slots as follows:

FIRST TIME SLOT (49 YEARS)

Daniel 9:25
Know therefore and understand that from the going forth of the word to restore and build Jerusalem to the coming of the anointed one, a prince, there shall be seven weeks.

SECOND TIME SLOT (434 YEARS)

Daniel 9:25,26
Then for sixty-two weeks it shall be built again with squares and moat, but in a troubled time. And after the sixty-two weeks, an anointed one shall be cut off, and shall have nothing; and the people of the prince who is to come shall destroy the city and the sanctuary. Its end shall come with a flood, and to the end there shall be war, desolations are decreed.

The first two portions of Daniel's prophecy cover the birth and crucifixion of Jesus and up to the utter destruction of the Temple by the Romans in 70AD. It is quite clear that a timeframe gap separates the first four hundred and eighty-three years of the total four hundred and ninety years of the prophecy. In other words, there is a further seven years that need completion after which the age will come to a close.

---

[29] Another interpretation of "seventy weeks of years" would be "seventy sets of seven weeks".

THIRD TIME SLOT (7 YEARS)

Daniel 9:27
He shall make a strong covenant with many for one week; and
for half of the week he shall cause sacrifice and offering to cease;
and upon the wing of abominations shall come one who makes
desolate, until the decreed end is poured out on the desolator.

It is quite clear from the prophecy that we are a people living in the gap years and that the last seven years are edging nearer. But it is logical to ask, why a time gap between the destruction of the Temple and the end of the age?

Why a time gap?

I suppose the quick answer includes "Why not?" "God has His sovereign purposes" and "God places clues in different parts of scripture that force us to go on a treasure hunt". God's word, the Bible, is rich in treasure, and the more we search its pages the deeper our treasure trove is. It leads us to the greatest treasure of all, the grace and mercy of God, the blood of the cross and eternal life in the kingdom of heaven.

We are constantly thrown upon a reliance on and faith in God. Our walk is a relational walk.

Another aspect to prophecy previously discussed is that prophetic events will not always occur consecutively. However, when we study Daniel's prophecy it soon becomes obvious that verses 25 and 26 talk about a period before the birth of Jesus, His birth and death and then on to the merciless destruction of the second Temple.

The gap period sees Jesus coming, and there is no better explanation for this than through these words:

John 3:16,17
For God so loved the world that he gave his only Son, that
whoever believes in him should not perish but have eternal life.
For God sent the Son into the world, not to condemn the world,
but that the world might be saved through him.

We are living in the time gap. The opportunity period given to us is clearly explained:

John 3:18
He who believes in him is not condemned; he who does not believe is condemned already, because he has not believed in the name of the only Son of God.

The third part of Daniel's prophecy deals with aspects that lead up to the second coming and the close of the age. When we place this prophecy alongside others, such as that of Ezekiel chapters 36 through to 39, it becomes clearer that certain things have to take place first, and we have discussed these during the course of this chapter.

A new heaven and a new earth

Having talked about the second coming of Jesus we are left with a final revelation where John says:

Revelation 21:1-4
Then I saw a new heaven and a new earth; for the first heaven and the first earth had passed away, and the sea was no more. And I saw the holy city, new Jerusalem, coming down out of heaven from God, prepared as a bride adorned for her husband; and I heard a loud voice from the throne saying, 'Behold, the dwelling of God is with men. He will dwell with them, and they shall be his people, and God himself will be with them; he will wipe away every tear from their eyes, and death shall be no more, neither shall there be mourning nor crying nor pain any more, for the former things have passed away.

The concept of a new heaven and a new earth is not new to the Jewish people. Isaiah speaks about a time of Messianic ecstasy and says:

Isaiah 65:17
For behold, I create new heavens and a new earth; and the former things shall not be remembered or come into mind.

In this new heaven and earth, those counted as righteous through the blood of the cross will forever leave behind old experiences and memories and worship God.

The circle will be completed. Genesis began with man living in unity and peace with God. Revelation sees the promised restoration of man living in perfect harmony with God. Sin will finally be utterly destroyed and righteousness will dwell. The coming of the 'new' Jerusalem will be the definitive of peace.

As we can see from this brief overview, putting the pieces of the jigsaw together is not particularly easy. But the message holds firm. Let's be ready, spotless and at peace. God is close to establishing His plans.

> **2 Peter 3:13-15**
> *According to his promise we wait for new heavens and a new earth in which righteousness dwells. Therefore, beloved, since we wait for these, be zealous to be found by him without spot or blemish, and at peace. And count the forbearance of our Lord as salvation.*

CHAPTER FIVE

God's Holy Convocations

Exodus 23:14
Three times in the year you shall keep a feast to me.

Seed thought

Everything we do should be a result of our gratitude for what God has done for us.

- Lauryn Hill

Introduction

At first glance this might seem to many Gentile Christian believers a very odd chapter to include in a book that has so far talked about end time prophecy, signs and preparations for the return of Jesus. Those who are from Jewish and particularly Messianic Jewish backgrounds, on the other hand, would no doubt immediately make the connections.

The explanation of the purpose of this chapter will be given in stages as we progress through the chapter. Suffice for now to say that the reason for including this topic is fivefold:

- The convocations are God-appointed, and so it is of value to see what they are.
- It is important for us to grasp the fact that these feasts are not simply commemorative appointments; they are also prophetic because they set before us God's agenda. It is the prophetic

understanding of these feasts that helps us to understand God's intentions.

- It is also important to constantly keep in our memory what God has done and will do for us.
- Understanding the Jewish people, their relationship with God, beliefs and spiritual journey, allows the Christian believer to give credence to and authenticate their faith and belief.
- Prophetically I am convinced that 2013 has a spiritual significance that connects the general content of this book and the feasts.

The motive for keeping certain things in our memory and reminding ourselves boils down to "lest we forget". The passage of time, new generations and pushing things to the back of our mind are all ways in which we can easily forget and bury at the back of our memory. When we forget and place things out of sight and out of mind we become prone to ungratefulness and lose sight of who and what we really are and should be. The act of remembering reconnects us. It is about learning, appreciation, avoiding mistakes and errors; *not doing* something that will lead to hurt and *doing* things that lead to good outcomes. It is about keeping at the forefront of our minds those things that are good and acceptable: the blessings of God, the victory of the cross and what Jesus achieved for us.

To illustrate what I mean, if the memory of Jesus had not been preserved and passed down it would have been lost – and where would we be today? Coming from (and of course influenced by) Jewish roots, the New Testament Christians kept the feasts or *hamoyadim,* a Hebrew word meaning 'seasons' or 'the appointed times', because they understood their original significance and, thankfully, they have preserved the memories.

Two of the main reasons why Christian believers do not understand the feasts today are:

- The passage of time, where the teaching and practice have been generally lost (though a growing revival is now taking place).
- The belief that some rigidly hold that says Christians are under the new covenant not under Mosaic Law and so they

are totally freed from the Old Testament teachings. Jesus did not abolish the law; He fulfilled it.

Unfortunately, although there is much truth behind this view, it is very often an oversimplification and sometimes misunderstanding of what the new covenant really means. It is true to say that the feasts are not important as far as salvation and walking in righteousness are ultimately concerned. But blessings abound as we honour God through what they represent. Using a modern vernacular we must not 'throw the baby out with the bathwater'.

I am not advocating a return to sacrifices and such rituals; I am also not advocating legalism and the strict observance of the feasts. I am saying that there is a richness of understanding of God and His purposes that many of us have missed. We do not have to literally celebrate the feasts, but we should understand them. They provide constant reminders of what God has done, provoke confession of our sins and repentance, and remind us of our forgiveness and atonement. There are many aspects of the Old Testament that point us to the new covenant and also to the end time plans of God.

We will come back to these points a little later as part of the general discussion. Though, as I have already indicated, it would probably be true to say that there is a reawakening of these appointed times among Christian believers as closer ties with our Messianic Jewish brothers and sisters are growing in these last days. As we progress through this chapter we will discover that the feasts and rituals were given to the Jewish people as prophetic signs that point to Jesus the coming Messiah. They point us to living in a right relationship with God. They point us to the perfect sacrifice of Jesus and the healing of our body, mind and spirit. They also tell us about the coming Holy Spirit and our privilege and right to live supernatural lives.

The problem for the Jewish people was that they did not understand these signs (and many still have not). As Isaiah prophesied, they did not recognize Jesus when He stood among them. They were spiritually blind. All this is changing.

As the Messianic Jewish and Gentile Christian believers forge closer links, a deeper understanding of what in particular the Jewish people actually believe and celebrate is pushing aside much of the misunderstanding and misinformation that has existed. Very few

Christian Gentiles really know about their worship, customs, lifestyle and calendar of feasts. The closer ties are gradually opening new insights and dropping the 'scales' from our eyes so that we can see more clearly God's intentions and purposes.

Talking of a calendar of feasts, many of us living in our hectic modern world may think that the idea of recording activities in a diary to remember events is a comparatively modern idea and invention, especially as we can now use devices that bleep reminders. Would it surprise you to know that God was well ahead of us in keeping a calendar and diary of events? The calendar was established in Genesis where we read:

> Genesis 1:14
> *Let there be lights in the firmament of the heavens to separate the day from the night; and let them be for signs and for seasons and for days and years.*

And again a diary of events is methodically listed in Leviticus chapter 23 where several specific times of remembrance with seasonal timings for God's people to meet with Him, and He with them, are specified.

These diary times were not meant to be the only times spent with God. Both Jewish and Christian believer should, as Paul reminds us, be in constant contact:

> Ephesians 6:18
> *Pray at all times in the Spirit, with all prayer and supplication.*

We are liberated to walk daily in all of God's intended purpose. To put this in context, our modern equivalent might be celebrating birthdays, anniversaries and similar events with our family. Putting the dates in our diary and celebrating these times does not mean that we stop spending day-by-day or constant time with our family. We do not walk away from husband or wife or children and say, "See you at the next celebration!" Neither should we walk away from God, nor say, "See you next church calendar event!"

Just as our calendar and diary have a specific purpose and use, so God's calendar and diary also have deeper significance than most Christian believers might realize.

With these opening thoughts in mind I have presented several layers or points as bedrock to build upon. Let's now begin by taking a closer look at these specific occasions and work toward understanding what they are actually all about.

Understanding the feasts

The first thing that we need to clarify is that although we make specific reference to feasts or festivals, actually the original text does not literally mean 'a feast' in the way that we use this word today. It may surprise many to realize that what is really being established are appointments or meetings, which have set agendas, times and places. Any 'feast' that may take place is celebratory but the main purpose is to keep the appointment. The implication for us today is to keep daily appointments with God.

More than this, each feast or appointment is actually a prophetic indicator of things that were (and are) to come. It is the understanding of these prophetic insights that not only makes sense of living under the new covenant but also the signs of the times. Writing to the Colossians Paul confirms this point and suggests that the feasts are "only a shadow of what is to come; but the substance belongs to Christ" (Colossians 2:17). What Paul was trying to say here is that it is not about man-made legalism; it is about Christ. This point is important because many have solely tied their thoughts about the feasts to man-made traditions or even the old sacrifices that – yes, it is true – some Jewish people would mistakenly like to re-introduce, and not to God's intended purpose.

What I am leading to is that the feasts actually present for us the salvation plan and prophecies that God put in place and of which Jesus said:

> Matthew 5:17,18
> *Think not that I have come to abolish the law and the prophets; I have come not to abolish them but to fulfill them. For truly, I say to you, till heaven and earth pass away, not an iota, not a dot, will pass from the law until all is accomplished.*

As we take a closer look at God's appointments and how they link with salvation plans and prophecy these points will become clearer.

Before I go further it might be worth re-iterating and taking careful note that it would be true to say that we do not need to limit ourselves to one particular time of the year, month or week to remember what lies at the heart of God's divine appointments. The 'seasons' do however have biblical relevance.

God said to Moses:

Leviticus 23:2
Say to the people of Israel, the appointed feasts of the Lord which you shall proclaim as holy convocations, my appointed feasts, are these.

The title to this chapter is God's Holy Convocations, which was a heading taken directly from this scripture. But what does convocation mean? The Hebrew word for convocation is *miqra* meaning 'a sacred assembly, a calling together or a rehearsal'. The Greek word is *ecclesia* meaning 'assembly', which later refers to the congregation or gathering of the Church. And the Latin root *convocare* means 'to assemble, call or come together for a unique reason'.

Of course we are enthusiastically reminded about our open access to God in the New Testament book of Hebrews where we read:

Hebrews 10:24,25
Let us consider how to stir up one another to love and good works, not neglecting to meet together, as is the habit of some, but encouraging one another, and all the more as you see the Day drawing near.

The feasts that we are talking about are not only opportunities to meet but specially appointed times that are rehearsals for what is to come. They are times of preparation for the main event. God is saying to the Jewish people that they must *rehearse* or *practise* each of the feasts.

I cannot stress these points too much. It is really important for Christian believers to understand the deeper significance of the Jewish feasts. They are loyally rehearsed at specific times. They act as pointers to what is to come. With this firmly in mind, let's take a look at God's appointed feasts (these are God's feasts not man's).

THE SABBATH[30] (LEVITICUS 23:1-3).

There are fifty-two of these days in the year which differ from any of the other appointments because the 'appointment' did not originate from the Jewish or Mosaic Law.

Leviticus 23:3
It is a Sabbath to the Lord in all your dwellings.

The Hebrew word *Shabbat* means 'to stop' or 'to rest'.

This is a day that was first established at the time of creation, and for this reason it is a day when our Jewish friends remember that God created the heavens and earth. But it is more than a day of memorial or remembrance; it is also a day of commemoration where the Jewish people honour their freedom from the slavery of Egypt. They solemnly and respectfully remember who He is, why they are worshipping, and give thanks for their freedom. Sadly these are often lacking in many of our churches, worship and thanksgiving.

The Jewish people view Shabbat as a precious gift from God and show their respect by committing it to Him, by refraining from activities that can otherwise be done during the rest of the week.

As we know from scripture, Jesus had to correct the misuse of Shabbat created by men's traditions and legalism where they thought they could gain righteousness through piety. But putting this to one side, the principle of refraining from unnecessary work was, and is still, maintained. Jewish people today do not refrain from work per se on the Sabbath. They refrain from activities that are not necessary.

Shabbat is typically celebrated from sunset on Friday to sunset (or just a little after) on Saturday. The reason for this finds its roots in how a day was actually measured from the beginning of creation. For example we read:

Genesis 1:5
...and there was evening and there was morning, one day.

To Jewish people, Shabbat is a day of joy, rest, prayer and spiritual refreshment. It is also a day when members of the congregation can have bestowed upon them the honour of publicly reading from the Torah.

---

[30] also known as *Shabbat*

As well as services at the synagogue Shabbat is spent with family and friends. Indeed if you have been to Israel you will see that when the day has ended the people come out with joy and celebrate.

The Christian church has generally lost much of the joy and refreshment that our Jewish friends know. It meets for an hour or two and we think all is well – we have given the day to God and done our bit. The Gentile Christian believer often forgets the words of Jesus who said, "The Son of man is lord of the Sabbath" (Matthew 12:8). It is a time to joyously remember that Jesus lives and actively celebrate that our sins are totally washed clean. Sadly, this aspect of church has almost entirely disappeared. Again we read:

> **Hebrews 4:9-11**
> *There remains a Sabbath rest for the people of God; for whoever enters God's rest also ceases from his labours as God did from his. Let us therefore strive to enter that rest, that no one fall by the same sort of disobedience.*

This is a time to come expectantly into the holy presence of God, to meet with Jesus and to rest in Him. It is a time to soak up His presence and find spiritual and physical renewal. If this is not happening then something is wrong.

It is a strange thing that many of our churches today only hold one service on a Sunday or they only have services on a Sunday morning with comparatively very little happening during the course of the week. There are one hundred and sixty-eight hours in a week, and many of our church buildings are only used for between an average of three to ten hours! And yet the Bible says:

> **Hebrews 10:24,25**
> *Let us consider how to stir one another to love and good works, not neglecting to meet together, as is the habit of some, but encouraging one another, and all the more as you see the Day drawing near.*

Under the new covenant there should certainly not be a decrease in hours meeting together. Sunday is not the only day that we should be meeting. These are the last days, and we should meet more often than ever before, stirring one another to love and good works. These works must glorify God, present the gospel, fulfill His purposes and bring people closer to Him. If our works are not achieving all of this then we may need to re-consider what we are doing.

The feasts are split into two parts:

- *The spring or early rain feasts.*
  These feasts point to Jesus and were dramatically fulfilled in His death, burial and glorious resurrection.
- *The autumn or latter rain feasts.*
  Here the feasts point us to the return of Jesus and the end of the age.

We shall first look at the spring feasts because all of these prophetic feasts have now been fulfilled and serve to remind us of God's mighty hand at work.

The spring feasts

THE PASSOVER[31] (LEVITICUS 23:4-14).

The Hebrew for Passover is *Pesach,* which covers a period of seven days because it also encompasses the Feast of First Fruits[32].

Leviticus tells us the time and date God has appointed for the Passover celebration saying:

> **Leviticus 23:5**
> *In the first month, on the fourteenth day of the month in the evening, is the Lord's Passover.*

The modern-day Jewish calendar first month is known as Nisan, which equates to the end of March and beginning of April on our Gregorian (also known as the Western or Christian) calendar.

The Passover refers to the exile of the Jewish people in Egypt, a time when Pharaoh refused to release them despite a number of warnings and broken promises. The Israelites received instruction to place some of the sacrificed lamb's blood over the doorposts and lintel of their homes as a sign that they were mercifully spared God's judgment. It is important to highlight that failure to obey this instruction would mean that they would suffer the same fate as the Egyptians.

This feast has significance to Gentile Christian believers because the date and time coincides not only with Jesus' crucifixion but also

---

[31] also known as *Erev Pesach* or *Ta'anit Bechorim* or Unleavened Bread
[32] also known as the *Omer*

the same hour slaughtered lambs were ready for the Passover meal that evening. Paul makes this link for us by saying:

1 Corinthians 5:7,8
Christ, our paschal lamb, has been sacrificed. Let us therefore, celebrate the festival, not with the old leaven, the leaven of malice and evil, but with the unleavened bread of sincerity and truth.

The leaven or yeast mentioned by Paul represents sin, and unleavened represents the fact that yeast is not present or, put another way, sin having been taken away. Just as the blood of the lamb 'saved' the Jewish people in Egypt from death so the blood of the lamb Jesus is our 'door' to salvation.

Effectively what we see here is that Jesus fulfilled the Old Testament prophecy of a lamb going to the slaughter. The feast was of course fulfilled under the new covenant when Jesus shed His blood and hung on the cross. Now when His blood sacrifice is willingly joined to the faith of a person, in Jesus the sinner is freely granted a pardon from the death penalty of sin and forgiven.

This leads us neatly into the feast of the Unleavened Bread, which according to God's diary is celebrated on the following day – 15th of Nisan:

Leviticus 23: 6
And on the fifteenth day of the same month is the feast of unleavened bread to the Lord; seven days you shall eat unleavened bread.

For the Jewish people it aptly celebrates their release from bondage. As we have already seen, the leaven or yeast represents sin. For the Christian believer Jesus was the perfect sacrifice who separates us from the bondage of sin. Peter states:

1 Peter 2:22
He committed no sin; no guile was found on his lips.

Again, John said:

1 John 3:5
In him there is no sin.

And yet again we read:

2 Corinthians 5:21
For our sake he made him to be sin who knew no sin, so that in him we might become the righteousness of God.

Under the new covenant our desire is to live holy lives as people who are washed clean by the blood of the cross.

Christian believers celebrate the feast of unleavened bread or the Passover meal in what we know as the Lord's Supper, Communion, Holy Communion or the Eucharist. The Passover meal is actually a symbol of the gospel message. Jesus said:

Luke 22:19,20
This is my body which is given for you. Do this in remembrance of me.' And likewise the cup after supper, saying, 'This cup which is poured out for you is the new covenant in my blood.'

Jesus very clearly says that the Lord's Supper is about remembering him.

Nisan also comes at the season of the latter rain; as does the feast of the First Fruits, which Jewish people remember as the time when they entered the Promised Land and gave an offering of the first fruits of the land. For the Christian believer the link here is with the resurrection of Jesus, and Paul connects this by saying:

1 Corinthians 15:20,21
Christ has been raised from the dead, the first fruits of those who have fallen asleep. For as by a man came death, by a man has come also the resurrection of the dead.

Jesus rose from the dead on the day of first fruits and so He fulfilled this prophecy to the day! A coincidence? No, God set His timetable in place from the very beginning. He has lain before us exactly what His plan is.

PENTECOST[33] (LEVITICUS 23:15-22).

The diary for this feast is carefully explained as follows:

Leviticus 23:15,16
You shall count from the morrow after the Sabbath, from the day that you brought the sheaf of the wave offering; seven full

---

[33] also known as *Hag Ha Shavuot*

> *weeks shall they be, counting fifty days to the morrow after the seventh Sabbath.*

For this reason Pentecost comes fifty days after the day of first fruits.

Pentecost (Acts 2:1) or *Shavuot* was also called the Feast of Harvest (Exodus 23:16), the Feast of Weeks (Exodus 34:22) and the day of the First Fruits (Numbers 28:26). It is Pentecost that links the promised coming of the Holy Spirit, and it was on this summer day the Christian church was supernaturally established in the upper room with one hundred and twenty disciples. The events leading to the first influx of members is stunningly recorded in these words:

Acts 2:41,42
There were added that day about three thousand souls. And they devoted themselves to the apostles' teaching and fellowship, to the breaking of bread and the prayers.

This event is also known as the 'early rain'. In Joel 2:28[34] we learn there will be a latter rain, an end time outpouring of the Holy Spirit. Just as the 'early rain' saw many saved so in the 'latter rain' many will come to salvation as God makes a last effort in His yearning as He is "not wishing that any should perish, but that all should reach repentance" (2 Peter 3:9). The implication for us today is to live supernatural lives – to live in a way that demonstrates who we are by the grace and mercy of God and to bring in a harvest of souls.

As I mentioned earlier, all of the spring feasts have now been fulfilled.

---

[34] "And it shall come to pass afterward, that I will pour out my spirit on all flesh; your sons and your daughters shall prophesy, your old men shall dream dreams, and your young men shall see visions." The coming of the Holy Spirit at Pentecost was God's last major intervention on earth. His representative is with us today to open the floodgate of heaven and bring revival. It is a shocking fact that many are squandering the opportunity divinely given to us; we turn our backs on revival and have no heart for it. Worse, we live outside of a daily supernatural lifestyle. A growing number of those in the church hold the form of godliness but deny its power (see 2 Timothy 3:5, KJV).

The autumn feasts

THE FEAST OF TRUMPETS (LEVITICUS 23:23-24)

Leviticus 23:23-24

And the Lord said to Moses, 'Say to the people of Israel, in the seventh month [Tishri], on the first day of the month, you shall observe a day of solemn rest, a memorial proclaimed with blasts of trumpets, a holy convocation.'

This day runs concurrently with *Rosh Hashanah*. This originally warned of Israel's impending judgment. For the Christian it heralds the return of Jesus because the Rapture and the trumpet blast are synonymous:

Matthew 24:31

He will send out his angels with a loud trumpet call, and they will gather his elect from the four winds, from one end of heaven to the other.

1 Thessalonians 4:16

The Lord himself will descend from heaven with a cry of command, with the archangel's call, and with the sound of the trumpet of God. And the dead in Christ will rise first; then we who are alive, who are left, shall be caught up together with them in the clouds to meet the Lord in the air; and so we will always be with the Lord.

This feast (the fifth out of seven) heralds the Rapture of the church.

We have already seen that God has set His agenda and plan of action. Events that took place in the Old Testament were similarly paralleled on the same date in the New Testament. I am not claiming anything here other than to say that a degree of logic would point to the second coming of Jesus taking place in the month of Tishri or September.

Rosh Hashanah (meaning 'beginning of the year') signifies the beginning of the Jewish New Year (Leviticus 23:23-25). It is a time of repentance, preparation for the Day of Judgment and prayer for blessing and fruitfulness.

Under the new covenant we are similarly called to live repentant lives, holy and blameless. We are lovingly called to prepare for the coming of Jesus.

THE DAY OF ATONEMENT[35] (LEVITICUS 23:27)

Leviticus 23:27
One the tenth day of this seventh month is the day of atonement.

Celebrated in September this is widely considered by Jewish people as the holiest day because it relates to the cleansing of sins and reconciliation with God. It again prophetically points us to the second coming of Jesus.

The significant importance of this day is perhaps best summed up in these words:

Zechariah 12:10
I will pour out on the house of David and the inhabitants of Jerusalem a spirit of compassion and supplication, so that, when they look on him whom they have pierced, they shall mourn for him, as one mourns for an only child, and weep bitterly over him, as one weeps over a first-born.

Oh, to have a heart that weeps over the sacrifice that Jesus gave; not to live in despondency but to live in the joy that this sacrificial act has created!

THE FEAST OF TABERNACLES[36] (LEVITICUS 23:34)

Leviticus 23:34
On the fifteenth day of this seventh month and for seven days is the feast of booths to the Lord.

Exodus 33:16
You shall keep the feast of ingathering at the end of the year, when you gather in from the field the fruit of your labour.

This is the last feast of the year. The booths are temporary dwellings that the Jewish people use during this feast time to remind them of the forty-year wanderings in the wilderness.

One of the most wonderful things about the wilderness wanderings is that the children of Israel lived daily in God's supernatural blessing for forty years. They had no shortage of food, water, clothing or direction. Every day was a supernatural day.

---

[35] also known as *Yom Kippur*
[36] also known as Booths, *Sukkot* or Ingathering

Just as God provided in a supernatural way for the Jewish people so we too can live daily in supernatural provision. We have the promise that "My God will supply every need of yours according to his riches in glory in Christ Jesus" (Philippians 4:19).

The feast of Tabernacles not only looks back but also forward to the kingdom of God and the multitude of white-robed tribulation saints described in Revelation 7:9-17.

The autumn feasts have not been entirely fulfilled yet. We are living in the latter rain era. Just as there is an ingathering of crops, so pictorially there will be an ingathering of souls with every true revival. We have seen this happening where pockets of revival have taken place but these have been tasters of what is to come. Just as the New Testament church saw thousands coming to the kingdom in one day so we too will see this during the latter-day harvest, before the 'rain' falls and the 'ark' door closes. This is, after all, what God intends.

I hope that this overview of the appointed feasts has shown that the underlying purpose of celebrating, or perhaps more accurately *remembering*, these 'feasts' is their prophetic preciseness and recognition of who God is. These are not just ancient Old Testament histories that 'died' at the coming of Jesus. They tell us about Jesus and the role He played, and plays, in God's purpose for humanity. These appointments have a purpose that unifies both Jewish and Gentile believers.

Yeshua, our peace and unity

The Church of Yeshua, of God's people, includes both Jew and Gentile. When Paul wrote to the church in Ephesus he said:

Ephesians 2:13-16

In Christ Jesus you who were once far off have been brought near in the blood of Christ. For he is our peace, who has made us both one, and has broken down the dividing wall of hostility, by abolishing in his flesh the law of commandments and ordinances, that he might create in himself one new man in place of the two, so making peace, and might reconcile us both to God in one body through the cross.

This statement by Paul is conciliatory, and so anyone who acts in a way contrary to this is acting against the peace and unity of Jewish and Gentile believers established through the cross of Jesus.

The eventual unification of the Jewish and Gentile believers through the cross does not leave the Old Testament null and void. Jesus did not abolish the Law or the prophets; He came to fulfill them (Matthew 5:17). The Greek word for fulfill is *pleroo* and means 'to make full, to fill up to full measure, to abound or supply liberally or to make complete'. What Jesus was really saying is that He was the cause, means or fulfillment of God's obeyed will. To put this in another way Jesus is the perfect measure and promoter of obedience. Jesus was the perfect remedy for the separation that occurred in the Garden of Eden and sins committed. He was the means of repairing the damage of sin, opening the 'door' of the kingdom and being the welcoming host for our return to God.

A further point to consider is found in Paul's words where he actually says to the Romans, "Do we then overthrow the law by this faith? By no means! On the contrary, we uphold the law." (Romans 3:31). The problem for many Christian believers actually centres on their understanding or misunderstanding of what exactly the Law is. There is a difference between the Law and the Commandments and what I will generally refer to as the 'ceremonial laws'.

Jesus most certainly did not come to abolish the Commandments, the prophecies of the prophets or His Father's prophetic appointments. Jesus did, however, fulfill the need of the ceremonial laws. For example, instead of sacrificing a lamb to seek reconciliation with God, Jesus became the perfect sacrifice. There is now no requirement for things like sacrifices, avoidance of certain foods or circumcision.

The Law makes us aware of our sin and the wages of that sin, but because of the blood of Calvary we can now be set free from its consequences and hold over us. We are no longer under condemnation. The law has its purpose and place. It shows us our sin. It can do no more than that. It is holy, pure and unmovable. Jesus did not come to remove the law and its ability to show who and what we truly are. He did however come to cleanse us so that our imperfections could be wiped clean. Once in this place the Law helps us to stay on track, and as we walk with Jesus, do as He did, so we walk closer to holiness and our reflection becomes more and more at one with the Law, and holy.

In fact the situation we should find ourselves in was succinctly expressed by the Psalmist who said, "I delight to do thy will, O my God; thy law is within my heart" (Psalm 40:8). The Law is positive, a means of keeping us on track and in obedience to God. In this sense it does not condemn; it 'pricks' our conscience to repentance and humility.

There are those who will argue that the grace of God means that Christian believers are no longer under any aspect of the Old Testament and the law. In addition to the fact that "all scripture is inspired by God" (2 Timothy 3:16), this argument often forgets that the grace of God, His unmerited favour, has been in evidence since time began. Grace is not something that just came with Jesus and the New Testament. What basis do I have for saying this?

The Old Testament book of Genesis emphasizes God's grace. Let's take a look at some of the examples given to us through:

- *Noah*
  "Noah found favour in the eyes of the Lord" (Genesis 6:8). The King James Version translates this verse as, "Noah found *grace* in the eyes of the Lord."
- *Lot*
  "Behold, your servant has found favour [grace] in your sight, and you have shown me great kindness in saving my life" (Genesis 19:19).
- *Moses*
  "I know you by name, and you have also found favour [grace] in my sight" (Exodus 33:12).

If you find yourself hesitant to celebrate biblical feasts, consider whether you follow your church or liturgical calendar and remember such seasons as Advent, Epiphany and Lent or specifically celebrate Christmas and Easter. Do you join in with Bonfire Night, Valentine's Day, Mother's and Father's Day, Shrove Tuesday or Halloween? Most of these celebrations find their roots in pagan festivities!

Should Christians celebrate the feast days?

The question really suggests a hint of legalism. It is not a simple matter of yes or no. The quick and simple answer to this question is, what is Jesus saying to you? Certainly there is no need for sacrifices and rituals. It is a question of heart purpose.

Writing to the Colossians Paul said:

> Colossians 2:16,17
> *Let no one pass judgment on you in question of food and drink or with regard to a festival or a new moon or a Sabbath. These are only a shadow of what is to come; but the substances belongs to Christ.*

> Colossians 2:20-22
> *If with Christ you died to the elemental spirits of the universe, why do you live as if you still belonged to the world? Why do you submit to regulations, 'Do not handle, Do not taste, Do not touch' (referring to things which all perish as they are used) according to human precepts and doctrines?*

These scripture verses correspond with Hebrews chapter eight and say that Christian believers should not allow any restriction by "human precepts and doctrines". Yet, how many of our churches are doing just this and caught up in artificial precepts, doctrines and traditions?

I was recently astounded to hear during the course of a sermon the preacher blatantly encouraging the congregation to look at, read and know the denominational doctrinal and rulebook as part of their Christian walk. My thoughts run quickly to "What about the Bible?" This did not get a mention! What has the church come to? No wonder we do not see God moving as we ought!

It is tragic to hear and see the Christian church engaging in historic anti-Semitic speech and attitudes. The misunderstandings and actions of the past should stay there: in the past. We cannot move forward whilst old wounds dwell and our hearts remain unforgiving.

The book of Hebrews informs us that the new covenant is superior to the old covenant. This is because Jesus has taken sins and washed them clean by His once-and-for-all sacrifice, His death for those who believe in Him and follow in total commitment to him. The Holy Spirit has implanted the law in the believer's heart. But, we are also told not to judge. For example Paul said:

Romans 14:5
One man esteems one day as better than another, while another man esteems all days alike. Let every one be fully convinced in his own mind.

Although the Christian church does not generally remember these feasts, understanding their significance unlocks the amazing parallels that are found between them, Jesus and the Christian walk; they give us invaluable insights into understanding the Bible that would otherwise be lost. There surely cannot be a problem with a Christian believer, if they so wish, taking time to remember some of the important feast days that were originally established in the Old Testament (remembering them in the same way that the early Church did). The problems exist where human precepts, doctrines and traditions override God's word and requirements. It is where the sacrifice of the cross is not fully understood, taught and lived by. It is about placing Christ in the centre of what we do, honouring God and giving glory to Him. It is not about celebrating the feasts per se.

Having said all of this, there are in fact three remembrance days that God called men to celebrate. So what does this mean for us, and should the church celebrate the feasts or not? To answer this question head-on and in simple terms, yes! We do not need to celebrate them in the traditional sense but rather to focus our attention on God, Jesus and the Holy Spirit. They help us to know who we are in God's plans, where we are going and to worship in Spirit and truth.

If we look at the early Church there were three feasts that Jesus and the disciples celebrated in addition to the Sabbath. These three feasts have never been revoked. They were originally established in the Old Testament and reiterated in the New Testament.

So what exactly are these important feasts and how do they fit with Jesus?

God's appointments with men

At the head of this chapter I highlighted Exodus 23:14, which says, "Three times in the year you shall keep a feast to me." Deuteronomy provides us with a little more information saying:

Deuteronomy 16:16-17
Three times a year all your males shall appear before the Lord your God at the place which he shall choose; at the feast of

unleavened bread, at the feast of weeks, and at the feast of booths. They shall not appear before the Lord empty-handed: every man shall give as he is able, according to the blessing of the Lord your God which he has given you.

We can see from this scripture that God has specifically called all men to the following feasts:

- The Feast of Unleavened Bread (The Passover; Exodus 23:15), reiterated by Jesus: "Do this in remembrance of me" (Luke 22:19). See also 1 Corinthians 11:23-32.
- The Feast of Harvest (Pentecost; Exodus 23:16). The Holy Spirit was given during the feast of Pentecost (Acts 2:1-4). The feast also celebrates the first fruits of harvest. When Jesus was resurrected from the dead he was described as the first fruit of the dead (1 Corinthians 15:20).
- The Feast of Ingathering (Tabernacles; Exodus 23:16). Jesus and his disciples celebrated this feast (John 7:1-13).

Leviticus speaks of "the appointed feasts of the Lord" (Leviticus 23:2). This means that these feasts are specially appointed and they are the Lord's. They are not men's! These 'appointments' have not been rescinded, so who are we to question them?

Before we take an even closer look at these feasts than we have so far it is interesting to note the words of Hosea who said:

Hosea 6:3
Let us know, let us press on to know the Lord; his going forth is sure as the dawn; he will come to us as the showers, as the spring rains that water the earth.

Why is this interesting? This is a call to press on, to do all we can to know the Lord, Jesus the Messiah. It is a prophetic statement; it says that Jesus will "come to us as the showers". The showers here are the autumn showers that come after the spring rains. Dear reader, it is not by accident that God's feasts take place during the spring and autumn seasons.

If we wanted assurance of God's feast callings we learn again from the text in Exodus that all the Israelite men (see Exodus 23:17) were specifically required to keep these appointments with God. It is a calling placed upon the heads of the house and family, the male leaders, to fulfill their God-given responsibilities.

As we take another look at these appointments it is important to keep in mind the role God has placed on men and not how society has changed or views this. It is not about being 'politically correct', and it is certainly not about reducing the vital importance of women. It is about obedience to God and bringing His ordained purposes forward so that love flows and the example that Jesus showed is carefully followed.

Many will not like this but Paul said, "The husband is the head of the wife as Christ is the head of the church" (Ephesians 5:23). The man has a leading role, a responsibility to walk as Christ walked and protect the household under the blood of Christ by teaching the blood of the cross and taking communion (Passover), being filled with the Holy Spirit (Pentecost) and covering the home by giving first fruits to God, confessing and repenting sins (Tabernacles).

Passover (Pesach) – fulfilled

This is the first feast on the Jewish calendar, a springtime feast and is, as we will discover shortly, symbolic of our salvation. It represents the beginning of our personal relationship with God.

Described in Exodus chapter twelve we find that Passover was first instituted because of Pharaoh's intransigence and refusal to obey God's word. Several warnings were given but Pharaoh would not heed these. Finally his stubbornness led to the 'pass over' of the angel who was sent to smite the firstborn in Egypt.

Pharaoh dealt harshly with the Jewish people. This persecution eventually led to an angel of the Lord releasing the Israelites. When we turn to the New Testament and the book of Acts, again chapter 12, we come across Herod's persecution of the church, the martyrdom of James and the miraculous release of Peter by an angel of the Lord. What makes this remarkable is that it too took place "during the days of Unleavened Bread" (Acts 12:3) – the unleavened bread being commemorative of the speed in which the Jewish people fled from Egypt. This is a period that I will discuss further shortly.

The traditional Passover celebration began with the high priest going to Bethlehem to collect a lamb without blemish. On his way back to Jerusalem the high priest passed through the East Gate on his way to the Temple where four days before and every day up to Passover he inspected the lamb. On the day of Passover the lamb (along with others from the nation) was ceremonially slaughtered by the high priest between 9am and 3pm in the afternoon, a period lasting six hours.

When we consider the events of Passover it soon becomes clear that they have similarities with Jesus. For example Jesus was born in Bethlehem, proclaimed as the lamb of the world (John 1:29) and lived a sinless life. In other words, He was like the lamb taken from Bethlehem and was without blemish. But as we follow the story further we discover that on His entry into Jerusalem riding on the back of a colt He entered through the East Gate. This entry into Jerusalem has become known as 'the triumphal entry'. Ezekiel prophesied that because Jesus entered Jerusalem via this route "this gate [East Gate[37]] shall remain shut; it shall not be opened, and no one shall enter by it; for the Lord, the God of Israel, has entered by it; therefore it shall remain shut" (Ezekiel 44:2). Today, any visitor to Jerusalem will clearly notice that the East Gate has indeed been bricked up and sealed. This gives us visual evidence of the reliability and authenticity of God's word as truth.

As we trace the parallel activity of the high priest who for four days inspected the sacrificial lamb we discover that for four days Jesus was mercilessly interrogated and beaten until on the day of Passover He was finally crucified. Hanging on the cross for six hours, from 9am to 3pm when He died, Jesus fulfilled this 'rehearsed' prophecy to the exact day and hour. The death of Jesus was the perfect sacrifice for the sins of humanity.

Today the Jewish people partake in a meal within their homes on the evening before Passover, known as the *Seder*. Some families also take part in this meal on the evening of Passover in faithful accordance with Leviticus 23:5,6 because Passover originally commenced from twilight on the fourteenth day of Nissan. This meal consists of certain foods that have symbolic relevance. An important part of this remembrance feast is the retelling of how God delivered the Israelites from the slavery of the Egyptians and set them free from their bondage – a story found in the Old Testament book of Exodus.

During the Seder meal four cups are used:

- The cup of sanctification.

---

[37] also known as the Golden Gate

- The cup of thanks.
- The cup of redemption.
- The cup of acceptance and praise.

The Last Supper was a Passover meal, where Jesus used the cups. Luke tells us that Jesus "took a cup [note this says *a* cup and not *the* cup], and when he had given thanks" (Luke 22:17) broke the bread, and holding the cup He said that "this is the new covenant" (the cup of redemption, the total remission of sins). The cup of redemption is what we use in Holy Communion.

For us today the story, or perhaps more accurately the *prophecy*, of Passover is a forerunner or picture of how God intended to save the world by releasing it from bondage and the death of sin. In the same way that the blood of the sacrificed lamb was liberally shed and smeared over the doorposts to save the inhabitants from death and release them from bondage, so it was that Jesus was also described by John the Baptist as "the Lamb of God, who takes away the sin of the world" (John 1:29). John the Baptist recognized Jesus as the perfect sacrifice for our sins. Just as only those Israelites who placed the blood over their doors were supernaturally saved so only those who will accept Jesus and follow Him will receive salvation. The blood of Jesus is the means by which the consequences of sin pass over us.

When Jesus said that He had come to fulfill the law (Matthew 5:17) we can now see from this example exactly what He meant and how He accomplished it.

As we have seen, Christian believers celebrate the feast of Passover in the form of Communion, Holy Communion or the Eucharist. Paul said:

1 Corinthians 5:7,8
Cleanse out the old leaven that you may be a new lump, as you really are unleavened. For Christ, our paschal lamb, [Passover Lamb] has been sanctified. Let us therefore celebrate the festival, not with the old leaven, the leaven of malice and evil, but with the unleavened bread of sincerity and truth.

We are called to partake of the Lord's Supper (Communion) in order to remember Jesus and what He achieved. We are called to do this in a repentant and worthy manner. Paul explained this point through these words:

> 1 Corinthians 11:27-30
> *Whoever, therefore, eats the bread, or drinks the cup of the Lord in an unworthy manner will be guilty of profaning the body and blood of the Lord. Let a man examine himself, and so eat of the bread and drink of the cup. For any one who eats and drinks without discerning the body eats and drinks judgment upon himself. That is why many of you are weak and ill, and some have died.*

Pentecost – fulfilled

Pentecost is the coming of the Holy Spirit and the birth of the Church. When we trace the history of the feasts it becomes clear that their timings on the calendar have also coincided with major Bible events.

Jewish people were celebrating Pentecost far before the New Testament Church.[38] When the Israelite nation was born and they received the Ten Commandments we read:

> Exodus 32:28
> *The sons of Levi did according to the word of Moses; and there fell of the people that day about three thousand men.*

About three thousand died because they had worshipped a golden calf. When the church was born Peter, filled with the Holy Spirit, stood and preached a powerful sermon. He concluded by saying:

> Acts 2:38
> *Repent, and be baptized every one of you in the name of Jesus Christ for the forgiveness of your sins; and you shall receive the gift of the Holy Spirit.*

About three thousand souls were miraculously added to the Church on that day. This is the role of the Church: to add souls to the Kingdom of God until the trumpets sound and the Rapture takes place.

How amazing God is! Nearly three thousand lost their lives because of idol worship and disobedience but nearly three thousand are saved because of repentance! What can we learn from this?

---

[38] The word Pentecost comes from the Greek word *pentecoste* meaning 'fifty' or 'fiftieth'. A contextual link with this term is found in Leviticus 23:15-22

On the day of Pentecost Jewish people read the account of Ruth. In this story Ruth represents the antithesis of hate, war and bloodshed. We find instead love, devotion and faith in the face of tragic circumstances, a love that breaks the rift between Jewish and Gentile people. Ruth is in fact an ancestress of Jesus who through the cross tore away separation between Jewish and Gentile people by His loving, selfless sacrifice – a sacrifice freely accessible through repentance and faith. Anyone who denies this or holds anti-Semitic beliefs or thoughts denies what Christ has done.

Jesus warned, "Be ready!" That means that we must repent of all known sins. We are to clear ourselves of anything and everything that will hinder us from becoming holy. In Leviticus we read:

Leviticus 11:44
I am the Lord your God; consecrate yourselves therefore, and be holy, for I am holy.

Not by accident, this is again repeated in Peter's first letter where he says:

1 Peter 1:14-16
As obedient children, do not be conformed to the passions of your former ignorance, but as he who called you is holy, be holy yourselves in all your conduct; since it is written, 'You shall be holy, for I am holy.'

This is a time to drop to our knees and ask God if there is anything that we need to get sorted between Him and us. Now is the time to commit totally to God and serve Him.

When Jesus returns He will be looking for a church "without spot or wrinkle or any such thing, that she might be holy and without blemish" (Ephesians 5:27). Again, in the book of Hebrews we read:

Hebrews 12:14
Strive for peace with all men, and for the holiness without which no one will see the Lord.

Our yearning should lead be for the tongues of fire to rest upon us in order that we might live supernatural lives and walk daily in holiness.

Tabernacles (Booths) – not entirely fulfilled

This feast is a picture of the future coming kingdom of God and the Millennial Reign[39]. Unlike the first two feasts mentioned in this section, this has not yet been fulfilled. What I mean here is that Jesus has partially fulfilled this prophecy through the cross. The coming of the Holy Spirit is part of the prophecy, and we are living in the wilderness period, gathering souls to the kingdom ahead of the finale, entry into the kingdom of heaven.

This feast is a reminder of the time that the Jews spent in 'booths' during their wilderness experience, a time when they were under the day-by-day protection and provision of God. It also coincides with the ingathering of crops, the end of the harvest gathering. It is a time of joy, a time to remember who God is and how great He is.

BACKGROUND INFORMATION

The Israelite return from exile coincided with the feast of Tabernacles. We learn that the governor Nehemiah and priest Ezra taught the people and they said:

> Nehemiah 8:9
> *This day is holy to the Lord your God; do not mourn or weep.*

It is for this reason this feast is a time of great joy and happiness. As we read further we find these words:

> Nehemiah 8:13
> *The heads of father's houses of all the people, with the priests and the Levites, came together to Ezra the scribe in order to study the words of the Law.*

From this study they discovered that Moses had commanded the people to dwell in booths during the feast. Again we understand why booths have become part of the celebration – serving also to remind the people of their dwelling place during the exile.

The central importance of this feast becomes clearer when we discover that it was during this exact time Solomon's Temple was solemnly dedicated to the glory and honour of God as described in 1 Kings 8:2:

---

[39] Revelation 20:1-10

154

All the men of Israel assembled to king Solomon at the feast in the month Ethanim, which is the seventh month.

This was a time when God was rightfully honoured and welcomed to live with us.

Coupled with these facts is that this was also a time in the year when ingathering took place, and so the produce of the field (Exodus 23:16), the fruits (Leviticus 23:39) and threshing floor and winepress produce (Deuteronomy 16:13) were collected. In addition to first offerings being given to God, the people also hung them in their booths as thanks and reminders of God's faithful provision whilst in exile.

The feast is a forerunner of the last days. It is a time to remember who God is and give Him His rightful place so that He 'tabernacles' (dwells) with us. It is a time when God is exercising His sovereign power over the disobedient. It is also a time to harvest souls before God brings His people into the eventual Promised Land, the kingdom of heaven.

What we are unraveling is a feast with huge implications. Zechariah in fact says that all nations should keep the feast of tabernacles:

Zechariah 14:16-19
Every one that survives of all the nations that have come against Jerusalem shall go up year after year to worship the King, the Lord of hosts, and to keep the feast of booths. And if any of the families of the earth do not go up to Jerusalem to worship the King, the Lord of hosts, there will be no rain upon them. And if the family of Egypt do not go up and present themselves, then upon them shall come the plague with which the Lord afflicts the nations that do not go up to keep the feast of booths. This shall be the punishment to Egypt and the punishment to all the nations that do not go up to keep the feast of booths.

The captivity and persecution of the Israelites in Egypt, the plagues, the blood over the doorposts, the wilderness experiences and God's covering of His people and the eventual coming of His people to the Promised Land now take on a new significance. These are a forerunner, a message conveying pictures of the last days and the coming land of 'fruit and honey'.

Light and water play an important part in this feast. The light refers to the 'glory cloud' or the 'pillar of fire' signifying the holy presence of God. Water of course refers to the parting of the Red Sea and the life-giving water that issued from the rock at Rephidim and Meribah described in Exodus 17:1-7 and Numbers 20:2-9.

Moving to the New Testament we read that on the last day of the joyful celebration of this feast Jesus spoke these words:

> John 7:37-39
> *If anyone thirsts, let him come to me and drink. He who believes in me, as the scripture has said, 'Out of his heart shall flow rivers of living water.' Now this he said about the Spirit, which those who believed in him were to receive; for as yet the Spirit had not been given, because Jesus was not yet glorified.*

Pentecost of course was the pouring out of the living word, the word of truth. Paul explained a little more about the rock of living water and said:

> 1 Corinthians 10:1-4
> *Our fathers were all under the cloud, and all passed through the sea, and all were baptized into Moses in the cloud and in the sea, and all ate the supernatural food and all drank the same supernatural drink. For they drank from the supernatural Rock which followed them, and the Rock was Christ.*

All had the same experiences. All saw God working miracles. All received God's provisions. But as we read further the next verse says:

> 1 Corinthians 10:5
> *Nevertheless with most of them God was not pleased; for they were overthrown in the wilderness.*

Even though all have the same opportunities, just as sin prevented some from entering the Promised Land so sin will prevent some from entering the kingdom of God. This thought has perhaps nowhere been better expressed than in these words:

> Psalm 1:2-6
> *Blessed is the man who walks not in the counsel of the wicked, nor stands in the way of sinners, nor sits in the seat of scoffers; but his delight is in the law of the Lord, and on his law he meditates day and night. He is like a tree planted by streams of water that yields its fruit in its season, and its leaf does not wither. In all that he does, he prospers. The wicked are not so,*

but are like chaff which the wind drives away. Therefore the wicked will not stand in the judgment, nor sinners in the congregation of the righteous; for the Lord knows the way of the righteous, but the way of the wicked will perish.

What I am saying here is that we need to keep our 'appointments' with God and maintain a right relationship with Him.

Under the new covenant the three 'remembrance feasts' or appointments are:

- The Lord's Supper (Passover) where we remember what Jesus has achieved on the cross.
- Receiving the supernatural fire of the Holy Spirit (Pentecost) and walking daily by the Spirit.
- Honouring, abiding and dwelling with God (Tabernacles). This is about living in daily readiness for the return of Jesus.

Before we leave this chapter there is one further celebration that no longer receives attention. Well you may ask, why bother with it? The reason for bringing this to our attention is its link both to faith and God's desire that we live holy lives.

The Sabbatical and Jubilee years

Background information about the Sabbatical (*shmita* meaning 'release') and Jubilee (*yovel*[40]) years can be found in Leviticus chapter twenty-five.

SHMITA

Shmita is also known as the sabbatical year or *sheviit*, which means 'seventh'. It runs on a seven-year cycle. The command of God says:

> **Leviticus 25:3,4**
> *Six years you shall sow your field, and six years you shall prune your vineyard, and gather in its fruits, but in the seventh year there shall be a Sabbath of solemn rest for the land, a Sabbath to the Lord; you shall not sow your field or prune your vineyard.*

The Leviticus command of God is to allow the land to rest.

---

[40] also written *yobel*

Observing this command is one that takes a great deal of faith in God. The command is literally to stop growing crops and vines for one year. It is to rely totally on God to provide in other ways. This is a picture of how we should be living our lives in faith for without it Hebrews 11:6 tells us that it is impossible to please God.

The question of course is how will the people survive? God gave this promise if the people would trust Him:

Leviticus 25:21,22
I will command my blessing upon you in the sixth year, so that it will bring forth fruit for three years. When you sow in the eight year, you will be eating old produce; until the ninth year, when its produce comes in.

What a promise! God says, "If you obey my words and trust me I will give you a bumper crop every sixth year." In other words God was guaranteeing enough provisions to live on for the period covering Shmita. Where obedience and faith are exercised, God supernaturally provides.

YOVEL

The Jubilee year is celebrated every fifty years. The timeframe for this is explained as follows:

Leviticus 25:8-10
You shall count seven weeks of years, seven times seven years, so that the time of the seven weeks of years shall be to you forty-nine years. Then you shall send abroad the loud trumpet on the tenth day of the seventh month; on the Day of Atonement you shall send abroad the trumpet throughout all your land. And you shall hallow the fiftieth year, and proclaim liberty throughout the land to all its inhabitants; it shall be a jubilee for you, when each of you shall return to his property and each of you shall return to his family.

Yovel is also known by other names. Isaiah refers to it both as The Year of the Lord's Favour (Isaiah 61:2) and the Year of Redemption (Isaiah 63:4) whilst Ezekiel calls it the Year of Liberty (Ezekiel 46:17). Each of these titles is descriptive of the holy celebration, which aptly commenced on the Day of Atonement.

This celebration is extra special because not only are the fields left fallow but all debts cancelled and slaves set free. It is a year when no wrongs would be committed against another and God would be feared. It is a time to get closer with God and to live in His Holy intent of love, forgiveness and obedience.

Jesus, reading from Isaiah chapter sixty-one, spoke about the Jubilee in these words:

Luke 4:18,19
The Spirit of the Lord is upon me, because he has anointed me to preach good news to the poor. He has sent me to proclaim release to the captives and recovery of sight to the blind, to set at liberty those who are oppressed, to proclaim the acceptable year of the Lord.

Jesus proclaimed a partial fulfillment of this celebration in that He has set man free from the bondage of sin and opened the way to the liberty of being called children of God. The eventual fulfillment of this celebration will of course be when Jesus returns.

Very few Jewish people now celebrate Shmita, and the Jubilee Yovel has not been observed for many centuries. The fact that Yovel has not been celebrated probably since as far back as 70AD means that counting the years to decide when the next date would fall today is not particularly easy though some indications may point to this being soon.

With all of this knowledge and understanding it begs the question, how and why did the Jewish people miss their Messiah when He was actually standing before them? And, given what is known today, why are many Jewish people still waiting for their Messiah?

In one sense it seems inconceivable that Jewish people have been so blinded, but it is equally true that much of the Christian church has become blinded to a great deal about God, Jesus and the Holy Spirit.

Probably the main reason the Jewish people did not recognize Jesus is concisely summarized in these words:

Matthew 15:3
Why do you transgress the commandment of God for the sake of your tradition?

Matthew 15:7-9
You hypocrites! Well did Isaiah prophesy of you, when he said, 'This people honours me with their lips, but their heart is far

from me; in vain do they worship me, teaching as doctrines the precepts of men.'

This statement says it all.

Yes, Jewish people know the Old Testament scriptures in a way that very few Christians know them. And yes, we should always be grateful to our Jewish friends for preserving scripture and the prophecies. But as Jesus said, they placed their own traditions and doctrines above God's word and taught these as truth. The Jewish people generally do not know the New Testament; after all, they do not accept Jesus and so their knowledge is incomplete.

Although the entire Bible is available to Christians, the church has fallen into the same pit as the Jewish people before us. In fact not only has it done exactly the same with man-inspired legalistic doctrines and traditions but also it has taken a step further with denominationalism, humanism, secularism and compromise.

Understanding the feasts lays a foundation upon which we can build, establish and live in harmony with God. We have not been set free to live under the new covenant and do as we please. We have been set free to humbly come into the holy presence of God, Jesus and the Holy Spirit. We have been set free to walk in holiness, peace and repentance. We have been set free to rightly handle the word of God, walk in the power of the cross and use the name of Jesus.

Our freedom has brought with it a spiritual responsibility.

Hebrews 2:1-3
Therefore we must pay the closer attention to what we have heard, lest we drift away from it. For if the message declared by angels was valid and every transgression or disobedience received a just retribution, how shall we escape if we neglect such a great salvation?

CHAPTER SIX

Knowing How to Get Ready

Romans 13:11,12
Salvation is nearer to us now than when we first believed; the night is far gone, the day is at hand.

Seed thought

God has a double purpose in redeeming us. On the negative side, it is to save us from hell—for which we should be eternally grateful. On the positive side, it is to prepare a people for Himself, who will share the throne with Christ. Before you read any further, pause for a moment and consider what it means to you personally, as a Christian, that you should be preparing yourself to reign eternally with Christ.

- Derek Prince[41]

Introduction

There is one thing we can constantly be certain about: if Jesus said, "Watch and be ready!" there is a reason He said it. If there was a reason for Jesus saying something then it is certain that we ought to know what that reason is.

Paul also warned about being watchful and he wrote:

1 Corinthians 16:13,14
Be watchful, stand firm in your faith, be courageous, be strong. Let all that you do be done in love.

---

[41] Derek Prince ministry letter 'Preparing to reign with Christ' (reproduced for free distribution).

161

With these thoughts in mind it seems logical that we should first understand what the Bible word for watch actually means. The Greek word is *gregoreo* and means 'vigilant, alert and awake, on guard, focused or watchful'.

So what exactly are we warned to guard against, be keenly vigilant about and watchful for?

Most of our churches have, and sadly still are, failing to prepare their flock, members or congregations for the second coming of our Lord and Saviour Jesus Christ. This book has been specifically dedicated to going at least some way toward filling some of the gaps in speaking about end time preparations and readiness. I for one definitely want to know what God is saying in these days and times we are living in. I do not want to rest on my laurels.

Paul reminds us:

> 1 Corinthians 13:12 (NLT)
> *Now we see things imperfectly, like puzzling reflections in a mirror, but then we will see everything with perfect clarity. All that I know now is partial and incomplete, but then I will know everything completely, just as God now knows me completely.*

A potentially disastrous stumbling block confronts some Christian believers. Whether or not you think we can or cannot lose our salvation it is far better to err on the side of safety – to constantly seek God, trust God, humble ourselves before Him, focus on Him and not think we know all that there is to know. When we die or Jesus returns it will be too late to argue about who is right and who is wrong. It will be too late if we are not ready.

It is a solemn fact that many Christians have become blasé about the second coming of our Lord. Many pastors and ministers of God do not consider this as an important message whilst others do not really understand it or its significance. Jesus, on the other hand, was very clear in His message and He said:

> Matthew 24:42-44
> *Watch therefore, for you do not know on what day your Lord is coming. But know this, that if the householder had known in what part of the night the thief was coming, he would have watched and would not have let his house be broken into. Therefore you also must be ready; for the Son of man is coming at an hour you do not expect.*

Yes, it is true that this message was given to the disciples of Jesus and every generation since has known that Jesus will return. Yes, generation upon generation believed the message and died not seeing it fulfilled in their lifetime. Those like in the parable of the ten maidens that were sensible kept themselves primed and ready. They allowed God to rule their heart. They followed the advice that Paul gave and became "imitators of God, as beloved children" (Ephesians 5:1). They made sure that they were in a right relationship with God.

The passage of time has however made many complacent, and few are truly living in the eager expectancy of an imminent Rapture. This situation, if it is one that any of us hold, is spiritually dangerous for at least two reasons:

- A lack of urgency leads to complacency and carelessness. In short, it leaves us off guard and open to attack and deception.
- As we see from the parable of the ten maidens, being unready is foolish to the extreme. Jesus left us with a warning to watch and remain ready.

Surely logic alone would tell us that if Jesus said, "Watch and be ready!" He meant watch and be ready! There must have been a very good reason Jesus made this statement. The logical question of course is: what exactly does this mean? We will tackle this question shortly.

There are others who 'bury their heads in the sand'. They do not want to think about the second coming. The thought is too scary. Yes, it is a scary thought. And yes, apprehension will fill us. It is after all an unknown experience. We do not, and cannot, really know what it will be like until it happens. We are only human; it is quite natural to have a mixture of feelings from apprehension through to excitement and elation. These holy fears need setting aside. They must not hinder us from preparing ourselves and looking with expectancy for Jesus to return.

It is time to voice something that many keep buried from view and live in self-denial over. There are those who in their heart lack belief about their salvation and the power of God. There is a denial of the return of Jesus because by doing this they can push to the background their confidence in being taken to heaven.

A fact of Bible prophecy is that Jesus is going to return for His Bride, the Church. There will be a wonderful marriage supper for the Lamb and we read:

Revelation 19:7,8
Let us rejoice and exult and give him the glory, for the marriage of the Lamb has come, and his Bride has made herself ready; it was granted her to be clothed with fine linen, bright and pure – for the fine linen is the righteous deeds of the saints.

Did you notice that message again: "his Bride has made herself ready"? When we think about attending a wedding we can draw a number of parallels with the message of making ourselves ready for Jesus to return.

Before the marriage and its celebration we spend time thinking about the gift that we can give. We go in search of that gift, and there is a cost involved. In our spiritual walk we think about what we can give through our faith. A faith without works is dead (James 2:14-26). Taking up the cross of Jesus brings with it a price – the price of denial of self and giving all of self to Jesus (Luke 9:23).

Getting ready for the big occasion takes time. It is not something that we can rush. We need to make sure that we have everything needed and that we are 'spotlessly clean' and perfectly presentable – arrayed in our best finery. Just as we take time to ready our self and look the best that we can for an earthly marriage, how much more time and effort will our spiritual marriage need?

We should live lives of expectancy: expectant of the fulfillment of God's promises; expectant that our daily walk with God is in His supernatural power; and expectant that Jesus is about to return for his bride.

The character of the Bride of Christ is nowhere better portrayed for us than in these words:

Ephesians 5:25-28
Husbands, love your wives, as Christ loved the church and gave himself up for her, that he might sanctify her, having cleansed her by the washing of water with the word, that he might present the church to himself in splendour, without spot or wrinkle or any such thing, that she might be holy and without blemish.

When Jesus returns He expects to find us living in holiness and without blemish – covered by His blood.

Without holiness we are uncompromisingly told "no one will see the Lord" (Hebrews 12:14). After the trumpet call it will be too late; Jesus will come for those that are ready. After all, He took great pains over telling us to get ourselves ready!

Jesus provided for us a parable comparing the kingdom of heaven with a marriage feast. It is worth taking a little time to look at this parable and see what we can learn from it.

Parable of the banquet and marriage feast

In Matthew 22:1-14 and Luke 14:15-24 two similar parables spoken by Jesus are carefully recorded. The parables are pictorially explained by Jesus who said:

Matthew 22:2
The kingdom of heaven may be compared to a king who gave a marriage feast for his son.

This is talking about God who prepares an invitation banquet or a feast for the marriage, the joining together of His son Jesus and the pure, holy Bride, the Church, the true believers, i.e. those that have committed themselves wholly to Christ, taken up their cross and faithfully follow him.

The purpose of these parables is twofold. First it warns the Jewish people because they refused the invitation to join the wedding celebration and so an opportunity for others to celebrate was given; the gospel was now opened to the Greeks and Gentiles. Second, the parables warn about worldly cares and concerns that crowd God out and make Him second choice.

We discover in the parable that in an audacious way three excuses or three cares of the world are smugly presented to God.

- Possessions
- Job / ministry / career
- Relationships

Let's take a closer look at the wider implications of these excuses.

Possessions

Luke records that the first invitee to the great banquet replied and said, "I have bought a field, and I must go out and see it; I pray you, have me excused" (Luke 14:18). Matthew tells us that the response to the wedding feast was that the people "made light of it and went off, one to his farm [his possessions]" (Matthew 22:5).

The attitude here is that possessions and money are far more important than God and far more important than the kingdom of heaven. This attitude forgets that "in the beginning God created the heavens and the earth" (Genesis 1:1); it forgets that "the earth is the Lord's, and everything in it, the world and all who live in it" (Psalm 24:1, NLT). The truth is, nothing we have is ours. We are born into the world with nothing and we die and take with us nothing. The grave in this sense is an equalizer. All material things that we have in life belong to God.

There is only one thing that we can acquire during our life and take with us into heaven. What we can get is a free gift given to us by God. It cannot be earned or purchased. Jesus put it this way:

John 14:6
I am the way, and the truth, and the life; no one comes to the Father, but by me.

John 3:16
For God so loved the world that he gave his only Son, that whoever believes in him should not perish but have eternal life.

Our true riches and possessions are not on earth and so we read:

Matthew 6:19-21
Do not lay up for yourselves treasures on earth, where moth and rust consume and where theives break in and steal, but lay up for yourselves treasures in heaven, where neither moth nor rust consumes and where theives do not break in and steal. For where your treasure is, there will your heart be also.

This life-changing choice is individually ours but sadly many have, and will, make light of it (Matthew 22:5).

Jesus also said that there will be those who may not make light of God's invitation but the 'magnetic pull' of possessions and riches will be so strong that they will not let go of them. This is explained in the parable of the rich young ruler found in Matthew 19:13-15, Mark 10:13-16 and Luke 18:15-17 which tells of a young man who kept the commandments, desired to follow Jesus, but he would not give what he had up and put God first. Jesus said, "It will be hard for a rich man to enter the kingdom of heaven" (Matthew 19:23b) but "everyone who has left houses or brothers, or sisters or father or mother or children or lands, for my name's sake, will receive a hundredfold, and inherit eternal life" (Matthew 9:29).

Jesus left us with this thought:

> **Matthew 16:26,27**
> *What will it profit a man, if he gains the whole world and forfeits his life? Or what shall a man give in return for his life? For the Son of man is to come with his angels in the glory of his Father, and then he will repay every man for what he has done.*

Getting ready means to put possessions in their place behind God or even, if necessary, to lay them down. Getting ready means to seek first His (God's) kingdom and His righteousness (Matthew 6:33) and, as Jesus requires, each of us should "deny himself [herself] and take up his [her] cross and follow me" (Matthew 16:24). If we have not reached these points we are not ready.

Job / ministry / career

The second excuse that we come across in these parables is, "I have bought five yoke of oxen, and I go to examine them; I pray you, have me excused" (Luke 14:19). Matthew tells us that having "made light" of the invitation the person went off "to his business" (Matthew 22:5).

When Jesus called His disciples He said, "Follow me." The response of those called was to leave what they were doing. They left their family and everything to follow Jesus. This point took on a spiritual significance after the rich young ruler walked away from Jesus with his head bowed low. Jesus turned to His disciples and said:

> **Matthew 19:24**
> *It is easier for a camel to go through the eye of a needle than for a rich man to enter the kingdom of God.*

Many have tried to complicate this scripture but actually the modern translation from Greek to English is correct.

The disciples immediately got the point, and we read that they were "greatly astonished" (verse 25) and asked, "Who then can be saved?" (verse 25). Jesus replied, "With men this is impossible, but with God all things are possible" (Matthew 19:26). This obviously sent the disciples into a 'spin' and a perplexed Peter said, "We have left everything and followed you. What then shall we have?" (verse 27). The disciples are then comforted as Jesus explains that by following Him and putting God first this action will bring reward in heaven.

Whatever job we may have, whatever career we may pursue or whatever our ministry, following Jesus comes first. Our relationship with God, Jesus and the Holy Spirit is far more important. We need to see the wider picture and not look at the limits of the here and now. What we can do ourselves is nothing compared with what we can do with God.

Jesus said:

> John 15:5
> *I am the vine, you are the branches. He who abides in me, and I in him, he it is that bears much fruit, for apart from me you can do nothing.*

We can try, we can strive and sweat tears and blood, but we will achieve nothing spiritually and supernaturally without Jesus. Yet with Jesus we can proclaim, as Paul did, "I can do all things in him who strengthens me" (Philippians 4:13).

There is no substitute for time spent in the word and prayer. It is also shocking that many churches now meet so infrequently. One comparatively short service on a Sunday is the sole commitment of many. Whilst talking about increasing the number of meetings one minister summed this up in words that went something like this: "People are busy; we cannot expect them to give more of their time."

The paradox of the Bible and God's call on our time is no better expressed than in these words:

> Matthew 6:33
> *Seek first his kingdom and his righteousness, and all these things shall be yours as well.*

Putting God first and taking the stress and anxiety out of our own efforts will lead to us having everything we need. The Psalmist made this statement:

Psalm 37:25
I have been young, and now am old; yet I have not seen the righteous forsaken or his children begging bread. He is ever giving liberally and lending, and his children become a blessing.

We do not *see* the supernatural in our lives because we do not *put* the supernatural into our lives.

Luke 1:37
With God nothing will be impossible.

Getting ready means to humble ourselves before God and put Him first. If we have not reached these points we are not ready.

Relationships

The third reason given for not accepting God's invitation is, "I have married a wife, and therefore I cannot come" (Luke 14:20) whilst in Matthew we read that matters were brutally taken a lot further: "the rest [of the people] seized his servants, treated them shamefully, and killed them" (Matthew 22:6). In these two responses we see the full spectrum of man's rejection of God from one extreme to another.

Jesus said that the first commandment is:

Mark 12:30
You shall love the Lord your God with all your heart, and with all your soul, and with all your mind, and with all your strength.

As we see, from the second commandment given by Jesus this does not mean that we do not love others and abandon them.

As we look closely at the first commandment we see that it is the Lord our God who we are to love "with all your heart". Indeed in Proverbs we also read:

Proverbs 23:26
My son, give me your heart, and let your eyes observe my ways.

It is about giving ourselves totally to God so that we stay fixed upon Him and not fixed upon another person and drawn away from Him. But why is this so important?

Apart from God wanting our full attention and love there is a very good reason that underlies this. When Moses was given the Ten Commandments it included these words:

Deuteronomy 5:7,8
You shall have no other gods before me. You shall not make for yourselves a graven image, or any likeness of anything that is heaven above, or that is on the earth beneath, or that is in the water under the earth, you shall not bow down to them or serve them.

This means that we must not idolize anything or anyone, including pictures or statues of Jesus. Idolizing anything or anyone takes our gaze off God. It not only displeases Him but it also leads us into spiritual danger zones.

Being drawn away from God is something that we are often warned about during the last days:

2 Timothy 3:2-5
Men will be lovers of self, lovers of money, proud, arrogant, abusive, disobedient to their parents, ungrateful, unholy, inhuman, implacable, slanderers, profligates, fierce, haters of good, treacherous, reckless, swollen with conceit, lovers of pleasure rather than lovers of God, holding the form of religion but denying the power of it.

It is this condition of man that leads to what we read in Matthew: the seizing, shameful treatment and even killing of God's servants.

We cannot be ready if we do not have our relationship with God, Jesus and the Holy Spirit in good order. In his first letter John says:

1 John 2:28
Abide in him, so that when he appears we may have confidence and not shrink from him in shame at his coming.

The Greek word for abide is *meno* meaning 'to remain with, stay with or abide with'. Today we might say 'to fellowship with'.

The call is for us to stay firmly focussed on God and not distracted by Satan's wiles and enticements. The story of Lot's wife is a chilling and stern warning about the failure of keeping our eyes on God. Due to their grave sin, God's wrath came upon the Dead Sea valley of Siddim and the cities of Sodom and Gomorrah. But because of his faithfulness the Lord was merciful to Lot and his family and allowed them to escape the judgment, warning them to flee and not look back. We then read these words:

Genesis 19:24-26

Then the Lord rained on Sodom and Gomorrah brimstone and fire from from the Lord out of heaven; and he overthrew those cities, and all the valley, and all the inhabitants of the cities, and what grew on the ground. But Lot's wife behind him looked back, and she became a pillar of salt.

Lot's wife was tantalizingly close to being saved and preserved but at the last moment she disobeyed, took her eyes off of God and looked back.

When the disciples asked Jesus when the end of all things will take place and what the signs will be He responded by saying, "Take heed that no one leads you astray" (Matthew 24:4) and, "He who endures to the end will be saved" (Matthew 24:13). In other words, we are not safe until we keep the faith to the end.

Jesus warned us to take heed of His words, to look for the signs, watch and be faithful. There are a number of New Testament scriptures that tells us about watching. Let's prayerfully consider each of these:

Matthew 26:41

Watch and pray that you may not enter into temptation; the spirit indeed is willing, but the flesh is weak.

Luke 21:34-36

Take heed to yourselves lest your hearts be weighed down with dissipation [carousing or indulging in physical pleasures] and drunkeness and cares of this life, and that day come upon you suddenly like a snare; for it will come upon all who dwell upon the face of the whole earth. But watch at all times, praying that you may have strength to escape all these things that will take place, and to stand before the Son of man.

1 Corinthians 16:13

Be watchful, stand firm in your faith, be courageous, be strong.

Ephesians 6:18

Pray at all times in the Spirit, with all prayer and supplication. To that end keep alert with all perseverance, making supplications for all the saints.

Colossians 4:2

Continue steadfastly in prayer, being watchful in it with thanksgiving.

1 Peter 5:8
Be sober, be watchful. Your adversary the devil prowls around like a roaring lion, seeking some one to devour.

There are times when God will leave us alone to watch, pray and stand firm. There will be times when those around us will isolate us as we seek to go deeper with God. We will have to wrestle like Jacob did if we want the blessings of God; our determination will need to prove that we will not let go until God grants His blessing and His supernatural power.

I could not hope to bring this chapter to a close in any better way than with the words of Peter:

2 Peter 3:1,2
I have aroused your sincere mind by way of reminder; that you should remember the predictions of the holy prophets and the commandment of the Lord and Saviour through your apostles.

Peter goes on to say that there will be scoffers who will ask, "Where is the promise of his coming?" (verse four). We must look expectantly for Jesus to return and make sure we live repentant lives. Peter urges that we consider what sort of person we should really be: [living] "lives of holiness and godliness, waiting for and hastening the coming of the day of God" (verses eleven and twelve).

Being ready means that we strive for holiness, peace and love. We must take care not to get caught up in the teachings of those who twist the scriptures to fit their own ends; we must preach the undiluted gospel message.

1 Peter 4:7
The end of all things is at hand; therefore keep sane and sober for your prayers.

CHAPTER SEVEN

Living the Last Days in Faith

Deuteronomy 6:4
Hear, O Israel: The Lord our God is one Lord.

Seed thought

Weak faith will produce a weak lifestyle. Limited faith will produce a limited lifestyle. Strong faith will produce a strong lifestyle and unlimited faith will produce an unlimited lifestyle.

We are what our faith is.

- Leon Gosiewski

Introduction

Why conclude this book with chapters on faith and belief? The reason is simple. During the course of this book we have discovered that over time some Christians have wrongfully criticised and turned their backs on the Jewish people. Jesus asked the question, "Why do you see the speck that is in your brother's eye, but do not notice the log that is in your own eye?" (Matthew 7:3). Hopefully this book has helped you to see the importance that God has placed upon Israel and the Jewish people in these last days. I pray that it has clearly sounded the preparation call. We are called to righteousness, holiness and love. Let's put our 'faith and belief' house in order.

It may seem odd to head this chapter on faith with the words, "Hear, O Israel: The Lord our God is one Lord" (Deuteronomy 6:4). The reason for doing this lies in the fact that this scripture is an

173

affirmation of faith that those of both the Jewish and Christian faiths agree upon.

Some Christian believers may be surprised to learn that the Jewish people pray this scripture verse twice each day (morning and evening) in what is known as the *Shema* (Hear). This prayed scripture verse is followed by the words *"Barukh shem kevod malchuto le'olam va'ed"* ("blessed be the Name of the glory of His kingdom forever and ever").

Our faith is in God, and yet very few understand faith as a vibrant, living and vital part of their lives and so truly live in faith. There is not only a misunderstanding of the closeness between Jewish and Christian believers that some have sadly sought to destroy or cunningly led to debase but also of faith in its practical daily outworking. It is not enough to speak about faith. Faith requires action.

It is time to throw off the man-inspired shackles of disagreement over unhelpful and faithless doctrines, precepts, traditions and cult groups. It is time to put on the cloak of true faith in God so that we fulfill the increasingly urgent commission placed upon us. The same should be said of us as it was of the early Church:

> Acts 5:14,15
> *More than ever believers were added to the Lord, multitudes both of men and women, so that they even carried out the sick into the streets, and laid them on beds and pallets, that as Peter came by at least his shadow might fall on some of them.*

A faith that is not rooted and grounded in God is unstable and tossed from one situation to another like a rudderless ship on a raging sea. It is a faith in doubt. Doubt will produce nothing but confusion, fear and misunderstanding.

Misunderstandings are probably one of the most common and damaging traits of humanity. When it comes to misunderstanding God's intents and purposes it is no different. Indeed it was the Jewish religious leaders' misunderstanding of who Jesus was that lay at the heart of His crucifixion. Pleading with His Father Jesus said:

> Luke 23:34
> *Father, forgive them; for they know not what they do.*

This was not only a prayer of forgiveness but also one of recognition that the people did not know what they had done.

Even with the benefit of hindsight and the passage of time since the death of Jesus, misunderstanding is still prevalent among Christian believers whether believer-to-believer or believer-to-God. It is staggering to think that Christians can engage in disagreements that can even become acrimonious over what often boils down to ambiguous and unimportant points of eschatology. And as we have discovered in this book even old wounds are kept open by misleading and harmful teaching. It is the heart of scripture that should surely be our unity in Christ. The root of this misunderstanding lies firmly in our lack of loving relationship with, and faith in, God.

To illustrate what I am saying about misunderstandings we read in scripture of occasions where Jesus was misunderstood as being an uncaring person even by those closest to him:

> Matthew 22:16
> *Teacher, we know that you are true, and teach the way of God truthfully, and care for no man; for you do not regard the position of men.*

> Mark 4:38
> *He was in the stern, asleep on the cushion; and they woke him and said to him, 'Teacher, do you not care if we perish?'*

> Luke 10:40
> *Martha was distracted with much serving; and she went to him and said, 'Lord, do you not care that my sister has left me to serve alone?'*

The negative aspects of these statements were boldly spoken against the well-known evidence of Christ's life. They did not show the true and known characteristic traits of Jesus and His compassion for people.

How easy it is for us to look at these examples that accuse Jesus of being uncaring and say we would not have done that! And yet, how many of us today immediately blame God for sickness, disease, disasters and calamities and yet also understand Him as the Creator and a God of love with whom nothing is impossible. Our God is a God of healing, miracles, life, honesty and integrity. Logic if nothing else should prove to us that God cannot put sickness or disaster upon anyone. Jesus highlighted this point for us when He said:

Matthew 7:11
If you then, who are evil, know how to give good gifts to your children, how much more will your Father who is in heaven give good things to those who ask him.

Nonetheless God endures the undeserved, unfair and unjustified blame for disasters and unhappiness. In reality blame should find its directed 'anger' at both Satan (and the horrible consequences of sin) and our own pride and obduracy. But why does God take the backlash of blame?

Apart from the multitude of clever deceptions and lies of Satan, who presses 'the right buttons' that incite our ego, inflate our sinfulness and much more besides, the truth of a situation or circumstance can also often become heavily disguised. Lack of knowledge can add to the confusion and difficulty. Spending insufficient time in the scriptures, in prayer and walking with God leave us bereft of understanding Him.

A clever trick to take focus away from Satan's involvement and ploys is to create misunderstanding. Where misunderstandings persist they gradually lead to disharmony and separation of mind and thoughts, or what we might generally call 'psychological separation'. Eventually, as the situations build up, this can then lead to relational (and for the Christian believer, spiritual) separation. All of this often starts from what seem to be innocuous beginnings that creep up slowly until they burst like the weak point of a water pipe placed under enormous pressure. But why does this all happen? I am sorry to say that answering this question is going to involve a great deal of courage and taking a large slice of 'humble pie'. The alternative is to maintain an entrenched attitude. This will lead to captivity and an unfulfilled life. The choice is ours individually to make.

Time for honesty

I wonder how many of you will be able to align yourself with my personal experiences. If honest, I have often viewed life from my own biased unloving and selfish perspective and not taken time to see or to find out the alternatives. Worse still, my arrogance has sometimes meant that I think I am right, and I do not want anyone to tell me or even prove to me otherwise. Armed with these imperfections, is it surprising that something is going to clash?

With great gusto and enthusiasm I have placed trust in God, but over time as things in life go wrong, brothers and sisters in Christ act in a way less than expected and pain is caused; God seems to go missing and prayers are not answered; doubts begin to arise. The day-by-day experiences do not fit the expectations, and as more time goes by frustration builds up. More doubts arise and gradually disillusionment sets in. This all leads in turn to a decline in trust and respect so that eventually communications break down as confidence is lost. Time spent with God wanes, and both the cares of the world and its enticements pull us away from God. We may even begin to listen to the skewed teachings and wisdom of men who say things like, "It was not God's will," trying to explain how one's faith in God is misplaced and discouraging us from looking to Jesus, "the pioneer and perfecter of our faith" (Hebrews 12:2).

When we throw into the mix our pride, lack of love and sinfulness as well as the clever ploys and deceptions of Satan we have a potentially volatile concoction. Looking down from the outside at these situations we might find many of them rather silly, egoistic and mercenary, so let's take a closer look at what is going on.

The Collins dictionary defines the word misunderstanding as "a failure to understand properly or a failure to sympathetically understand correctly"[42]. A failure to understand can either be attributed to poor communication, lack of communication or lack of knowledge. A failure to sympathetically understand may prove indicative of not taking the time to understand or being self-righteous. Whatever the cause we can so easily miss the point. Dealing with misunderstandings is the easiest and yet the hardest thing that we can do. It boils down to our willingness to accept that a misunderstanding is resolvable if we will work at it. Arrogance that will not admit we may have possibly concluded wrongly completes the downward spiral.

The Bible has much to say about acceptance of others, but the fact is if we fail to love as Christ loves we will not break through. Let's take a moment to prayerfully consider some helpful scriptures:

---

[42] Reproduced from Collins English Dictionary and Thesaurus with the permission of HarperCollins Publishers Ltd. © HarperCollins Publishers 1990. Collins ® is a registered trademark of HarperCollins Publishers Ltd. Collins English Dictionary and Thesaurus (1990) ISBN 9780004331869

1 Corinthians 13:4-7
Love is patient and kind; love is not jealous or boastful; it is not arrogant or rude. Love does not insist on its own way; it is not irritable or resentful; it does not rejoice in wrong, but rejoices in right. Love bears all things, believes all things, hopes all things, endures all things.

Ephesians 4:33,32
Let all bitterness and wrath and anger and clamour and slander be put away from you, with all malice, and be kind to one another, tender-hearted, forgiving one another, as God in Christ forgave you.

Philippians 2:3
Do nothing from selfishness or conceit, but in humility count others better than yourselves. Let each of you look not only to his own interests, but also to the interests of others.

If we fail to build a personal loving relationship with God we will not understand His ways and methods. In the Old Testament book of Proverbs we read these insightful words:

Proverbs 3:5-8
Trust in the Lord with all your heart, and do not rely on your own insight. In all your ways acknowledge him, and he will make straight your paths. Be not wise in your own eyes; fear the Lord and turn away from evil. It will be healing to your flesh and refreshment to your bones.

Neatly packaged in these few wise words we discover how each one of us can live in health and vitality.

We tend to view things from our own understanding. Pride and arrogance lead us to think that our wisdom is superior. Lack of humility dissipates genuine love and forgiveness. And selfishness sees our interests as being more important than those of others. As a result we become 'deaf' and 'blind' to reality. In the worst scenarios we may refuse to admit or even entertain that we might be wrong in our conclusion. God ceases to take centre place in our life. This entrenched position now begins to lead to anger, resentment and unforgiveness.

Love and walking in the Spirit must form our base, but if we are not rooted and grounded in faith, difficulties can easily lead to doubt.

As part of his soliloquy the little known Old Testament prophet Habakkuk received this response to a question that in various situations and circumstances I am sure many of us have also asked in one way or another: why does it seem the case that the more wicked punish, oppress or gain an advantage over the less wicked? God's response includes this statement:

Habakkuk 2:4
Behold, he whose soul is not upright in him shall fail, but the righteous shall live by his faith.

Whatever the outward appearance may seem, God is in control and the wicked will not succeed. In writing the first Psalm, the Psalmist understood this principle and concluded by saying:

Psalm 1:5,6
The wicked will not stand in the judgment, nor sinners in the congregation of the righteous; for the Lord knows the way of the righteous, but the way of the wicked will perish.

It would be true to say that living uprightly and by faith does not guarantee an 'easy ride' through life and, yes, sometimes the ungodly seem to get an advantage or 'upper hand'. But the life of uprightness and faith will always lead to eventual victory. No matter what may happen in life the truly upright live by faith in God and enjoy His good pleasure.

God promises that He will cater for all the needs of His people, and He has never failed in this promise. We are moving into an era where God's supernatural provision will now be supplied in greater abundance to meet His end time plan. We cannot afford to entertain even a hint of separation from God however this may manifest itself. Every true Christian believer must turn toward God's face in humility and prayer.

The Old Testament book of Chronicles was originally known in Hebrew as *Dibrey Hay-Yamin*[43] which means 'acts of the days' or in today's language we might say 'a daily record of events or happenings'. The reason why I have mentioned this here is because of some words contained in Chronicles (which incidentally was originally a single book) that are relevant to our daily events and happenings today. The chronicler recorded these words of God:

---

[43] or *Dibrey Ha'Yamin*

2 Chronicles 7:14
If my people who are called by my name humble themselves, and pray and seek my face, and turn from their wicked ways, then I will hear from heaven, and will forgive their sin and heal their land.

'Living to live' begins here.

On three occasions in the New Testament those often quoted words or sentiments that we looked at in Habakkuk 2:4 are again referred to in various ways:

Romans 1:16,17
I am not ashamed of the gospel; it is the power of God for salvation to every one who has faith, to the Jew first and also to the Greek. For in it the righteousness of God is revealed through faith for faith; as it is written, 'He who through faith is righteous shall live.

Galatians 3:11
Now it is evident that no man is justified before God by the law; for 'He who through faith is righteous shall live' [some manuscripts say "the righteous shall live by faith"].

Hebrews 10:37-39
'For yet a little while, and the coming one shall come and shall not tarry; but my righteous one shall live by faith, and if he shrinks back, my soul has no pleasure in him.' But we are not of those who shrink back and are destroyed, but of those who have faith and keep their souls.

'Living to truly live' means that eternity is life with God. What we see from these scriptures is that God is only pleased with those who live uprightly and by faith in Him. So what am I trying to say in these opening thoughts?

Living to please God

There are two significant ways that every one of us can live our lives in such a way as to please God. The corollary to this of course is that there are two ways to live one's life and displease God.

The first aspect of pleasing God is aptly summarised through these words:

Romans 8:8
Those who are in the flesh cannot please God.

180

The context of this verse is found in the encouragement for us to live in holiness, to live in the Spirit and not in the flesh. The term 'live in the flesh' means being dominated by our sinful nature or having cravings that incite sin. The reason why living in the flesh is so displeasing to God is again summarised as follows:

Romans 8:7
The mind that is set on the flesh is hostile to God; it does not submit to God's law, indeed it cannot.

The word for hostile in the Greek is *echthra* meaning 'enmity or hatred'. Now I do not know about you but for me the meaning of this scripture has suddenly been placed into a very different context. Being hostile can simply mean opposed but it does not necessarily indicate opposition born out of malice or hatred; it could merely indicate differences such as opposing politicians or opposition of competing athletes. Hostility in this context is softer than hatred and enmity. For this reason it is easy to miss the full impact of what this scripture is actually saying.

God is not looking for enmity; He is looking for sanctity. We are called to "be holy, for [He is] holy" (Leviticus 13:44). But this will take a determined effort on our part. The famous English Baptist preacher and author Charles Haddon Spurgeon (1834-1892) said:

You will not gain holiness by standing still. Nobody ever grew holy without consenting, desiring, and agonizing to be holy. Sin will grow without sowing, but holiness needs cultivation. Follow it; it will not run after you. You must pursue it with determination, with eagerness, with perseverance, as a hunter pursues his prey.[44]

Holiness is not sinful man's natural trait, but it is the intended norm of the Christian walk with God.

The second way for us to please or displease God is found through these words:

Hebrews 11:6
Without faith it is impossible to please him.

Faith in God is an outward demonstration of our total trust and confidence in the Creator with whom nothing is impossible. He

---

[44] *preceptaustin.org/holiness_quotes.htm*

181

cannot lie and He cannot fail us. Letting go of self and letting God take control of our lives means that He is free to work in us as He wills. The opening verse that heads this chapter makes the same point but in a different context, when Jesus said:

> **Matthew 10:39**
> *He who finds his life will lose it, and he who loses his life for my sake will find it.*

It is about our willingness to humbly submit to and trust God.

Let me 'cut to the chase' and 'pin my colours to the mast'. I cannot express the belief that I hold any better than the famous English evangelist of faith Smith Wigglesworth, who said:[45]

> *If it is in the Bible, it is so. It's not even to be prayed about. It's to be received and acted upon. Inactivity is a robber, which steals blessings. Increase comes by action, by using what we have and know. Your life must be one of going on from faith to faith.*

There are three key things that I would like to highlight from Smith Wigglesworth's statement:

- "If it is in the Bible, it is so."
- "Inactivity is a robber..."
- "...going on from faith to faith."

If it is in the Bible, it is so

The premise upon which this book has been written is that the Bible is the word of God. When Paul wrote his second letter to Timothy he said:

> **2 Timothy 3:16,17**
> *All scripture is inspired by God and profitable for teaching, for reproof, for correction, and for training in righteousness, that the man of God may be complete, equipped for every good work.*

This scripture verse starts with a word that is often either forgotten in discussions and debates about the Bible, or its importance lost from our thinking. I am of course referring to the word 'all'.

---

[45] *A Man Who Walked With God;* George Stormont; published by Harrison House, 1989

When I searched my dictionary for the meaning of the word 'all' it said, "the whole quantity or amount of"[46]. That seemed fairly conclusive, but just to make certain I searched the Greek word used in this context and discovered that it is the word *pas* meaning 'all, each, every, everything, the entire'. My conclusion is that all means all: every scripture, none left out, God inspires all of it. I am not trying to be offensive or clever but rather to show the point. There is no picking and choosing what we do and do not accept as God's word. It is the entire Bible.

The inclusiveness of the Bible got me thinking, what about this word inspired? The Greek word used here is *theopneustos* meaning 'inspired by God'! Let us take the opportunity to take a deeper look at the context of what Paul was actually saying to Timothy as part of his defence of the faith.

The setting is amidst a warning of the coming of apostasy where some turn away from and reject the Christian faith and the need to preach the truth of the Christian faith. Almost inevitably, the question arises about Jesus and the reliability of the scriptures.

Does the 'inspiration' of the scriptures mean that God dictated the words, and so no errors exist, or did writers write freely but with the Holy Spirit safeguarding against errors? Alternatively did the freedom of the writers and the various translations allow errors to creep in? What people asking these questions forget is that God is God. It is God who has made the scriptures available to us. The Bible is God speaking directly to us. "If it is in the Bible it is so."

There is more to consider. God cannot lie. God's promises are unchangeable. If He makes a promise He will never break it. In the letter to the Hebrews we read:

Hebrews 6:17,18
When God desired to show more convincingly to the heirs of the promise the unchangeable character of his purpose, he interposed with an oath, so that through two unchangeable things, in which it is impossible that God should prove false, we

---

[46] Reproduced from Collins English Dictionary and Thesaurus with the permission of HarperCollins Publishers Ltd. © HarperCollins Publishers 1990. Collins ® is a registered trademark of HarperCollins Publishers Ltd. Collins English Dictionary and Thesaurus (1990) ISBN 9780004331869

who have fled for refuge might have strong encouragement to
seize the hope set before us.

God's truth is immutable. It is our sure hope. Paul expressed this point to Titus when he wrote:

Titus 1:2
In hope of eternal life which God, who never lies, promised ages
ago.

If God never lies, our confidence that He inspires all scripture is totally assured. Our confidence can also be extended so that what we are reading in the Bible is not only what God wants us to read but to know and to live by.

Inactivity is a robber

If we do not act on God's word we will lose sight of it. Distractions, false promises made by man misinterpreting scripture, procrastination, sin, unbelief, our ego and lack of knowledge of God's love for us are some of the many reasons why we fail to walk with God in the way we should.

Dealing with the practicalities of faith James explains that it should always be demonstrably shown through our actions. Pulling no punches He says:

James 2:20
Do you want to be shown, you shallow man, that faith apart
from works is barren?

The King James Version translates this verse as:

But do you want to know, O foolish man, that faith without
works is dead?

The words 'shallow' (RSV) and 'foolish' (KJV) are translated from the original Greek *kenos* meaning 'empty, devoid of truth or vain'. James is clearly staggered that anyone could suggest having faith in God would not radically turn a person upside-down. True faith according to James must prove itself by producing noticeable evidence of its flow in a person's life. I wonder what James would make of our churches and most of us today. Would he see the proof of our faith in what we do and say?

During a recent visit to a church it was intriguing to read in the notices that they were holding House Group meetings and the subject they were going to study was "the healing gifts of the Spirit". One of the church members kindly took time to speak with me and asked about me. As part of my response, and having read the notices, I simply, in passing, mentioned my interest in the healing ministry. The comment that followed took me by surprise. This dear jovial woman immediately and firmly replied, "I am okay; I have my operation booked!" Of course, up until this moment I did not know that she was due to undergo an operation, but she made it clear that she was not open to further discussion. Her firm response to the fact that I mentioned healing ministry was sadly typical of faithless responses that I have met on many occasions.

Interestingly, only the week before I was talking with a minister of another church to thank him for his service. Although not relevant to what we had talked about, this dear brother suddenly began to talk about healing, and partly quoting from John 14:12 he said that Jesus had said, "You will do the same works as me, and greater works will you do." This statement was quickly followed by the comment that "of course, we do not know what Jesus meant when He said 'greater' works; we could never do anything that is greater." I explained that what this verse actually meant was we would do more works in number. The English word greater in Greek is the adjective *megas* meaning 'mass, measure of number or larger'. This clearly does not relate to greater miracles because by its own definition a miracle is a miracle!

It transpired that this dear brother had read one of my books, and he went on to make his personal views known to me saying God heals as He wishes, it is not about blockages of faith preventing healing, some receive healing who do not have faith. I explained that, yes, by the grace of God this is true. In some instances it is the faith of the person praying that brings God's healing touch. But Jesus also said to some who had put their trust into some form of action, " *Your* faith has made you well" (Mark 10:52). In the case of Christian believers there is an expectation to exercise our faith. There is always an exercise of faith, even if it is directly from God Himself. Someone somewhere had faith and exercised that faith through their actions.

The fact is, faith without action is of no more use than an electrical appliance that has not been plugged into the mains supplies. Of course, even this is not enough because the appliance must also be switched on! Indeed James explains his outburst by saying:

James 2:21-23
Was not Abraham our father justified by works, when he offered his son Isaac upon the altar? You see faith was active along with his works, and faith was completed by works, and the scripture was fulfilled which says, 'Abraham believed God, and it was reckoned to him as righteousness'; and he was called the friend of God.

Abraham was totally confident in God. He did not necessarily understand what God was doing but he implicitly trusted God – not just in word of faith but in positive action of faith. This trust earned Abraham the accolade as a friend of God.

It is of no value to have faith and fail to show this or, as James put it, "a man is justified by works and not by faith alone" (James 2:24). Our faith is powerfully activated through our words and our obedience.

The action of speaking

Speaking about the power of faith Jesus said:

Mark 11:22-24
Have faith in God. Truly, I say to you, whoever says to this mountain, 'Be taken up and cast into the sea.' And does not doubt in his heart, but believes that what he says will come to pass; it will be done for him. Therefore I tell you, whatever you ask in prayer, believe that you have received it, and it will be yours.

The principle expressed here is that what we believe and say is what we get. What we say is the expressive action of our belief.

If there is a mismatch between our faith and what we say the words we speak will take precedent. We have been uniquely created in such a way that what we think is what we say and what we say is what we do and what we do is what we become. What we do represents our works. What we become represents our life. Faith cannot be released without actions.

The action of obedience

The faith demonstrated by Abraham is succinctly described in these words:

Hebrews 11:8
By faith Abraham obeyed when he was called to go out to a place which he was to receive as an inheritance; and he went out, not knowing where he was to go.

Abraham demonstrated his faith by acting in obedience. He did as God asked even though he had no idea where he was going! He was totally confident that God had made a promise and God would be true to His word.

When King Saul disobeyed God Samuel delivered this message:

1 Samuel 15:22,23
Has the Lord so great delight in burnt offerings and sacrifices, as in obeying the voice of the Lord? Behold, to obey is better than sacrifice, and to hearken than the fat of rams. For rebellion is as the sin of divination, and stubbornness is as iniquity and idolatry. Because you have rejected the word of the Lord, he has also rejected you from being king.

Disobedience will separate God from us. But God will always honour an act of obedience. When faith is connected to the act of obedience we have the creation of a powerful and dynamic force.

The action of believing

We act in harmony with our beliefs. For example, if we believe that a chair will take our weight we will not hesitate to sit on it. Alternatively if we do not believe that a chair will take our weight doubts arise and we will either avoid it completely or carefully test it to satisfy our confidence.

When confronted with God's word and His promises we will either both believe it and trust it implicitly or doubt will arise and we will hold back. Doubting and holding back from trusting God are evidence of unbelief.

Every time we hold back and do not activate our faith we openly show our lack of belief and we become faithless. When Jairus received the news that his little daughter had died, before he could say anything Jesus said, "Do not fear, only believe" (Mark 5:36).

Doubt and fear produce unbelief. The clear message from Jesus was "only believe".

If our relationship with God and knowledge of His love are missing we will be unable to build a trust with Him. Talking about the certainty of faith arising from our love and obedience toward God we read in the first letter of John:

> 1 John 5:14,15
> *This is the confidence which we have in him, that if we ask anything according to his will he hears us. And if we know that he hears us in whatever we ask, we know that we have obtained the requests made of him.*

Smith Wigglesworth proved over and again that if we only believe great moves of God and miracles follow. He said: [47]

> *If we believe, we will have absolute rest and perfect submission. When God has entirely taken charge of the situation, you are absolutely brought into everything that God has, because you dare to 'only believe' what He says.*

Christian believers are both disempowered and rendered dull and ineffective through unbelief and inactive faith; or empowered, made alive and highly effective through belief and active faith.

Going on from faith to faith

Paul wrote:

> 2 Corinthians 5:7
> *We walk by faith, not by sight.*

There are times in life when everything around us seems to collapse 'around our ears'. Everything seems to go wrong. We cannot do right for doing wrong. Criticisms flourish and everything we seem to touch or do just falls apart in front of our very eyes. Even what we say is effortlessly taken wrongly or misconstrued, and we call out to God, "Where are you?" But as if to compound the problem God remains silent and things seem to get worse and not better.

---

[47] Taken from *Greater Works* by Smith Wigglesworth. Copyright © (1999) by Whitaker House. Used by permission of Whitaker House. *www.whitakerhouse.com*

Take heart my friend; this is not new. The Old Testament book of Job is both a picture of what suffering is and how faith always wins through. The opening verse of Job says:

Job 1:1
There was a man in the land of Uz, whose name was Job, and that man was blameless and upright, one who feared God, and turned away from evil.

If we are honest there may be besetting sins, disobedience, and lack of trust or poor choices in our lives that we can point to and understand why situations may have occurred. In our example of Job he is "blameless". All seems well. Job is in God's favour and prospers. What could go wrong? The answer? Satan tests Job's resolve to extremes that most of us could not even imagine.

Here is an upright man suffering extreme losses, and what does he do? We come upon an amazing verse in scripture – one that uncovers the character of Job and reveals the heart of a man of faith. He has lost much in his life. Those closest to him criticize and God remains silent and in the background. We would probably give up or apportion blame on others or even upon God. Job comes to God and he asks:

Job 7:20 (KJV)
Have I sinned? What have I done to You, O watcher of men? Why have you set me as your target, so that I am a burden to myself?

This is not a cry of unbelief and loss of faith in God. On the contrary, this is a cry from a man of faith asking if he has inadvertently offended his God in some way. You see, as far as Job was trustingly concerned, the problem could not possibly be with God. There had to be another explanation. Of course we have the benefit of knowing that the accuser, Satan, was behind the scenes causing mayhem, as he has and always will.

We see this same faith in God again and again in Job:

Job 13:15 (KJV)
Though he slay me, yet will I trust Him.

Job 19:25,26 (KJV)
I know that my Redeemer lives, and He shall stand at last on the earth; and after my skin is destroyed, this I know, that in my flesh I shall see God.

Nothing will deter Job from trusting His God and he eventually proclaims:

Job 42:2 (KJV)
I know that you can do everything, and that no purpose of yours can be withheld from you.

So, why did this happen to Job, and how could he state so clearly and boldly that God can do everything? This is probably best explained by James who said:

James 1:2-4
Count it all joy, my brethren, when you meet various trials, for you know that the testing of your faith produces steadfastness. And let steadfastness have its full effect, that you may be perfect and complete, lacking in nothing.

Again we read in the first of Peter's letters:

1 Peter 1:6,7
In this you rejoice [Peter speaks here of the treasure of our salvation laid up for us in heaven], though now for a little while you may have to suffer various trials, so that the genuineness of your faith, more precious than gold which though perishable is tested by fire, may redound to praise and glory and honour at the revelation of Jesus Christ.

Our trials both build character and test the genuineness of our faith – a faith that is more precious than gold and purified in the fire of God so that we can become more Christ-like.

When we trust God through the trials that we face, God sees and says, "Now I see your faith!" This is the faith that will stir God to move mountains. The exercise of our faith is often a long and lonely experience, but the exercise of faith produces within an individual the increased confidence to develop faith.

The loneliness of the long distance faith runner

Some years ago I read a well-known book called 'The Loneliness of the Long Distance Runner' by Alan Sillitoe (1959). In a similar way that Alan Sillitoe painted the picture of a lonely long-distance runner emerging from the morning mist and trudging across the undulating countryside so we can draw a parallel with the Christian running the course of faith. It can often, as those who tread this path know, be lonely, tough going and sometimes difficult to see ahead in the mist of time and problems.

The Apostle Paul said:

1 Corinthians 9:24
Do you not know that in a race all the runners compete, but only one receives the prize? So run that you may obtain it.

Again we read:

Hebrews 12:1
Let us run with perseverance the race that is set before us.

The spiritual race that any would-be faith runner undertakes is one of loneliness, endurance, perseverance and even occasional heartache. When asked during a televised London Olympic BBC report (2012) what it takes to win gold, double gold medallist Mo Farah said:

It's the grafting and hard work ... One hundred and twenty miles, week in, week out ... Long distance is a lonely event.

When you take up the race of faith it is a long road and few join you. Few understand what you are doing and why such deep discontentment of the 'ordinary' Christian life burns in your soul. Often there are no others to share with – even God can seem far off as you stride out in faith. There is nothing to hang on to other than your faith. Running the long distance race of faith means that you trust and believe even when all seems against you. The deep mire of life tries to suck you into its clutches. You feel unable to carry on and you cannot see the way out. The steep and seemingly impossible hill faces you shouting, "Stop!" It is impossible. Even God remains silent, and what you have hoped for seems no closer now than when you first began. Faith causes you to look to Jesus and to stay the course.

Faith is not about looking at the problems and difficulties. Faith is about looking into the eyes of Jesus. It is about being "filled with the fullness of God" (Ephesians 3:19). When in faith we are firmly focused on Jesus and filled with God's fullness the power of God will work in us and we will know the living truth of these words:

Ephesians 3:20,21
Now to him who by the power at work within is able to do far more abundantly than all that we ask or think.

Understanding faith

Hebrews 11:1,3
Faith is the assurance of things hoped for, the conviction of things not seen ... By faith we understand that the world was created by the word of God, so that what is seen was made out of things which do not appear.

Faith is not about what is going to happen sometime in the near or far future. Faith is what *has* happened; it is what is now in the present. Faith based upon what could happen is always going to be faith that could happen sometime but it will never be true faith because it's always going to be what *could* happen. Faith is a convicted assurance. It is the hope of receiving that which is not seen.

God sees what is now. He calls into being that which is not as if it were. Standing in faith is seeing what God sees in the present. When we ask for something in faith we need to see God as the God of miracles, the God of the impossible, the God of the present. If we do not see God this way we will not connect with Him.

Jesus said:

Matthew 7:7,8
Ask, and it will be given you; seek and you will find; knock, and it will be opened to you. For every one who asks receives, and he who seeks finds, and to him who knocks it will be opened.

There is no doubt or hesitation. When we ask we will receive. When we seek we will find and when we knock it will be opened. All of this will only happen if we encompass the revelations of God and see as He sees.

Isaiah 53:5
He was wounded for our transgressions, he was bruised for our iniquities; upon him was the chastisement that made us whole, and with his stripes we are healed.

Healing has already taken place. We have to see what we asked for in the light of what has already taken place. We cannot separate our faith vision from our life; the two should become one. We have to walk in God's dimension and only believe.

Oh, the times when I have tried to share with others about the depths of faith and they have just looked at me as if I were 'off the wall'! Or they have come back with comments such as, "We see in a mirror dimly," or, "It depends on how you interpret scripture," or, "You are too deep in your thinking." Yes, all true, but the pursuit of running in faith is a desolate place; you keep going no matter what it seems to be like – or you give up. If you keep going, eventually the light will come on, the power flows and you run with God. But oh, what a difficult place you have had to come through. How many times you have been utterly broken, moulded and bent in the hands of God!

Smith Wigglesworth once said:[48]

Great faith is the product of great fights.

Never can you rely on what appears to be through the eyes and senses – only by faith.

Hebrews 11:1
Faith is the assurance of things hoped for, the conviction of things not seen.

---

[48] *www.thegoodnessofgod.com/Wigglesworth.pdf*

CHAPTER EIGHT

Living the Last Days in Belief

1 Thessalonians 5:23
May the God of peace himself sanctify you wholly and may your spirit and soul and body be kept sound and blameless at the coming of our Lord Jesus Christ.

Seed thought

Your belief determines your action and your action determines your results, but first you have to believe.

- Mark Victor Hansen[49]

Introduction

Faith and belief are often used interchangeably to mean the same thing. In this sense it is very difficult to distinguish any difference between the two or talk about one without the other. As we learned from the last chapter, faith is about having confidence. But this begs the question, confidence in what or whom?

Mark 11:22 help us to understand where our faith should actually be directed by saying, "Have faith in God." The Christian faith is in God. It is in no one or nothing else.

Hebrews 11:1 defines faith as "the assurance of things hoped for, the conviction of things not seen". Faith in God leads to an assurance about the things we hope for even though we cannot see it.

---

[49] *www.getmotivation.com/mvhansen.htm*

Belief is about our attitude of mind. It is what drives our actions and the habits that make us who we are. It is for this reason that in Mark 11:23 we read:

Mark 11:23
...and does not doubt in his heart, but believes that what he says will come to pass.

We behave in accordance with our heart belief. If we believe we can do something we will keep going until it is finally done. If we do not believe we can do it, we will give up almost before we started.

Put simply, faith is about directing our lives toward and filling ourselves with God. It is about an implicit trust and confidence in God that is so assured that it does not doubt Him. Belief is about what lies in our heart and is expressed in what we say and do. What we believe can build us up or tear us down. It is for this reason that I have included this chapter.

One of the biggest threats hanging over the outworking and growth of a Christian believer's faith like a dark storm cloud is complacency. Complacency is like 'thorns' in the Christian believer's side and foot. Their poisons debilitate and blind the person to a need for change and growth. Eventually complacency breeds contempt shown through, for example, a disregard of (or disobedience to) God's commands, an alliance with worldly things, mediocrity, compromise, and contentment.

It may prove particularly unpleasant for some to hear, but a disobedient, mediocre, compromising and content Christian believer will never know the fullness of God's plans, intentions and purposes. A disobedient, mediocre, compromising and content Christian will never walk in the fullness of God's power and live to really live. Why do I say this? Let's take a moment to humbly and prayerfully consider these scriptures:

Proverbs 1:32
The simple are killed by their turning away, and the complacence of fools destroys them.

Zephaniah 1:12 (KJV)
And it will come to pass at that time that I will search Jerusalem with lamps, and punish the men who are settled in complacency, who say in their heart, 'The Lord will not do good, nor will He do evil.'

Revelation 3:15,16

I know your works, that you are neither cold nor hot. I could wish you were cold or hot; so then, because you are lukewarm, and neither cold nor hot, I will spew you out of my mouth.

I can sense some readers thinking that none of the terms I have used or scripture examples apply to them. Of course, this may be true – but has the impact and danger of complacency been fully grasped?

Referring again to the Collins dictionary it defines complacency as "smugness or extreme self-satisfaction"[50]. The dictionary.com definition says:[51]

A feeling of quiet pleasure or security, often while unaware of some potential danger, defect, or the like; self-satisfaction or smug satisfaction with an existing situation, condition, etc.

The Christian faith should inspire hope and concern to walk in the ways of God and please Him. It is about trusting implicitly in God and relying upon Him.

What I am trying to say is that complacency has no place in the Christian believer's life. Let's take a closer look at some of the reasons why complacency is such a deadly 'disease':

- Stops growth
- Stops prayer
- Stops belief

Complacency stops growth

When we feel self-satisfied and secure we can become content. There are many Christian believers – in fact I believe that it is the majority – who have fallen into this pit of Satan's clever deception. Sitting back with our feet up and smugly thinking that we have 'made it' only serves to make us ineffective. Smith Wigglesworth was a little more forthright and said, "If you do not progress every day you are backsliding."[52] To backslide means to move away from God.

---

[50] Reproduced from Collins English Dictionary and Thesaurus with the permission of HarperCollins Publishers Ltd. © HarperCollins Publishers 1990. Collins ® is a registered trademark of HarperCollins Publishers Ltd. Collins English Dictionary and Thesaurus (1990) ISBN 9780004331869

[51] *dictionary.reference.com/browse/complacency*

[52] *www.lit4ever.org/smith4.html*

I have often been taken by surprise at the 'wall of resistance' one meets in the Christian community. Often the right words are convincingly said or written but the action belies this. All sorts of excuses or arguments are destructively placed in the way and hinder progress. If honest I find it frustrating and hampering. There must surely be more than we are generally seeing and experiencing. There must surely be a vibrant expectation and fluidity of the actual presence of Jesus that we have yet to tap into.

I am not claiming to have made it, but rather this is about sharing my longing to fellowship with those of like mind. It is about encouraging those of like mind to push frustrations to one side, keep looking expectantly to Jesus, "run with perseverance the race that is set before us, looking to Jesus the pioneer and perfecter of our faith" (Hebrews 12:1,2), and break free from the imposed corporate shackles.

Some readers may be asking, what am I really talking about here? The best way I can explain these points is to turn to the beginning of Revelation chapter three and the message sent to the church in Sardis:

> Revelation 3:1-3
> *I know your works; you have the name of being alive, and you are dead. Awake, and strengthen what remains and is on the point of death, for I have not found your works perfect in the sight of God. Remember then what you received and heard; keep that, and repent. If you will not awake, I will come like a thief, and you will not know at what hour I will come upon you.*

What a terrible indictment: "you have the name of being alive, and you are dead." The problem is that this applies to the overall majority of churches, and yet they have become so blinded by their complacency that they actually think all is okay. The message is to wake up and salvage everything that we can, to get back on track with Jesus before it is too late.

The Christian believer's attitude should always be 'whatever it takes', 'all for Jesus', and a humility before God that says, "Do with me as you will." Instead of 'driving the car of life' and steering in directions that we want, it is about handing the 'steering wheel' over to God and allowing Him to take us to His chosen destination. Yes, it is a scary thing to do. And yes, we will no longer be in charge of our destiny. We will no doubt be taken out of our comfort zone, and it may cost much. Only the brave and committed will take this courageous step. If you choose not to let go, please do not hinder those who want more of God.

From the very time that Jesus died on the cross, the Christian believer has been consistently encouraged to live in a way that expects His return. We should constantly be living in daily expectancy. We should live in such a way that we are ready and know that Jesus will be totally pleased with what we are doing. In truth the state of the church in this country and the increasing secularism, humanism and complacency expressed mean that we are more dead than alive. Missionaries coming to us are even now evangelizing us!

Talking of his hope in attaining resurrection from the dead Paul said:

> **Philippians 3:12-14**
> *Not that I have already obtained this or am already perfect; but I press on to make it my own, because Christ Jesus has made me his own. Brethren, I do not consider that I have made it my own; but one thing I do, forgetting what lies behind and straining forward to what lies ahead, I press on toward the goal for the prize of the upward call of God in Christ Jesus.*

Standing still was not an option for Smith Wigglesworth or the Apostle Paul and it shouldn't be an option for us either.

Speaking against complacency in the Christian's walk the 'Mother of the Salvation Army' Catherine Booth (1829-1890) said:[53]

> *Many do not recognize the fact, as they ought, that Satan has got men fast asleep in sin and that it is his great device to keep them so. He does not care what we do if he can do that. We may sing songs about the sweet by and by, preach sermons and say prayers until doomsday, and he will never concern himself about us, if we don't wake anybody up. But if we awake the sleeping sinner he will gnash on us with his teeth. This is our work – to wake people up.*

The overwhelming longing to see more of God, more of His power at work in and through us should drive us forward – ever hungry and thirsty for more of God and what He has to give to us. It

---

[53] *www.evanwiggs.com/revival/portrait/redfield.html*

is a constant surprise to me that this is not where many believers dwell in their thinking.

'Swimming against the tide' is not an easy thing to do. I know from my own limited experience that Christian brothers and sisters can sadly be so cruel and uncompromising in their attitudes and speech when you stand up and say something different or challenge things as they are. When speaking out about the lost power of the church or watered down sermons, I've been accused of criticizing.

Wanting more from God can often be a painful experience. It is not a journey that one undertakes lightly or without courage, sacrifice and determination. There is a certain loneliness and despair that causes holy grief and tears as one throws oneself down at the mercy of God. I cannot express what it is like to plead before the mercy seat. Only those who have stepped this way can know the desperation for something that only God can grant, and paradoxically when He grants it, it will never be yours; it will only ever be His.

To have a burning desire for more of God is the only way to grow, flourish and truly 'live to live' as God intends.

Complacency stops prayer

"I am doing just fine, thank you." This is the type of comment that a complacent person will give. The sense of urgency diminishes, corners are cut, and riding on past success are just some of the many attitudes that complacency breeds.

When we become complacent in our prayer life and relationship with God we begin to tread a very slippery and sloppy downward slope. Joshua encountered sloppy complacency when he made an unwise covenant treaty with the inhabitants of Gibeon. He, along with his leaders, was craftily sucked into their web of lies and deceit. We read:

Joshua 9:14
So the men [Joshua and the leaders] partook of their [Gibeonite] provisions, and did not ask direction from the Lord.

Being deceived by the Gibeonites was not a trap that they had to fall into, but the Israelites got overconfident and failed to ask God. They thought that they did not have a need for Him and so they did not pray. Joshua was finding out that we could never take God for granted.

When we become self-centred we become blasé and complacent. We lose both our dependency on God and humility toward Him. When we stop praying we cease to believe.

Quoting from Isaiah 56:7 and Jeremiah 7:11, Jesus said:

Matthew 21:13
My house shall be called a house of prayer; but you make it a den of robbers.

When we look at the state of the church today, how much time is actually spent in prayer? From personal experience I estimate that the churches (includes various denominations) I have visited in recent months spent well under 10% of the service in prayer, most being about 3%. Many churches do not hold mid-week prayer meetings, but where these are held the percentage of church members attending is very small.

James reminds us:

James 4:2,3
You do not have, because you do not ask. You ask and do not receive, because you ask wrongly, to spend it on your passions.

The Greek word for ask is *aiteo* meaning 'to long for, to crave, to beg for'. This is not simply an asking; it is a pleading before God in such a way that our genuine, godly wish is earnestly expressed. James in fact goes on to explain that selfish pleading is made out of wrong motives.

Complacency stops belief

A complacent spirit relies on its own ability. It is proud, arrogant and self-reliant. These traits oppose humility and dependency.

God is calling His people to rid themselves of complacency. We must constantly be ready. The parable of the ten maidens is about preparing, being ready and watching for the coming of Jesus. We are clearly told, "Five of them were foolish, and five were wise" (Matthew 25:2). The foolish maidens were complacent. The parable tells us that they went to meet the bridegroom with lamps that had no oil. They did not believe that it was necessary to prepare. They thought that they would be able to share the oil carried by the wise maidens or buy what they needed at the last moment but it was too late.

The wise maidens were not leaving anything to chance. They prepared themselves, believing that although they did not know when the bridegroom would arrive, the bridegroom *would* come and they would be ready to meet him.

We receive from God because we actively believe that we will receive from Him. Our expectancy is to receive, and so we *will* receive. Jesus said:

> **Mark 9:23**
> *All things are possible to him who believes.*

The Greek word for believes used in this statement is *pisteuo* meaning 'to think something is true, to be persuaded that something is true or to place one's confidence in'.

Why belief is important

When we truly believe God and His promises they become truth in our inner thoughts and spirit. To put this another way, our beliefs decide what we accept as truth and this forms the mental attitudes that express how we consequently act. If we do not act in harmony with what we say we believe, we do not in reality believe it. It is for this reason that actions are more powerful than words. It is for this reason that faith without works is dead. It is for this reason that we read these very strong words in John's first letter:

> **1 John 4:20**
> *If anyone says, 'I love God,' and hates his brother, he is a liar; for he who does not love his brother whom he has seen, cannot love God whom he has not seen.*

The behaviour does not mirror the claimed love because what lies deep within any one of us will always show itself outwardly.

The Bible sometimes refers to this depth of belief as 'believing in your heart'. For example:

> **Romans 10:9,10 (emphasis added)**
> *If you confess with your lips that Jesus is Lord and <u>believe in your heart</u> that God raised him from the dead, you will be saved; for man believes with his heart and so is justified, and he confesses with his lips and so is saved.*

The heart is a symbol not only of our physical life but also of our spiritual life. In this verse we learn something that is very important to understand: "man believes with his heart".

It is for this reason that God waits to see what is actually in our hearts. The Psalmist expresses this point in the following example:

Psalm 17:3 (KJV)
You have tested my heart; you have visited me in the night; you have tried me and have found nothing; I have purposed that my mouth shall not transgress.

Again we read how God tested Hezekiah:

2 Chronicles 32:31
And so in the matter of the envoys of the princes of Babylon, who had been sent to him to inquire about the sign that had been done in the land, God left him to himself, in order to try him and to know all that was in his heart.

What is in our heart, what we truly believe, and consequently how we act, are proof of our commitment to God.

It is what lies deep within our hearts that will surface. Our beliefs decide our behaviour. We act in accordance with those things we believe in our heart, the centre of our spiritual life; and because we confidently believe, 'self' will be taken out of the equation and reliance on God takes its place. It is the highest form of trust and submission.

Trust in the Lord

In Proverbs we read:

Proverbs 3:5-8
Trust in the Lord with all your heart, and do not rely on your own insight. In all your ways acknowledge him, and he will make straight your paths. Be not wise in your own eyes; fear the Lord, and turn away from evil. It will be healing to your flesh and refreshment to your bones.

Paul said:

2 Corinthians 1:20
All the promises of God find their Yes in him.

What Paul meant was that we can totally rely upon God. The Greek word for 'yes' used in this verse is *nai* meaning 'assuredly'. All God's promises are guaranteed through Jesus. This point was dramatically confirmed by Jesus who made this incredible statement:

John 14:12-14
Truly, truly, I say to you, he who believes in me will also do the works that I do; and greater works than these will he do, because I go to the Father. Whatever you ask in my name, will do it, that the Father may be glorified in the Son; if you ask anything in my name, I will do it.

On many occasions when these scriptures are quoted, verse 12 is 'detached' from verses 13 and 14. Actually these verses come as a package; "he who believes in me" should never be separated.

The courage of our conviction is clearly demonstrated through our assured belief in Jesus. This belief will open the door for us to do the works that He did. Why? When we confidently use the name of Jesus from a base of convicted belief it will stir Jesus to do what we ask and produce supernatural outcomes.

Many Christian believers are happy to quote these words:

1 John 4:4
He who is in you is greater than he who is in the world.

Most of us do not however actually believe these words and live in the daily reality of them. If we did then sickness would not exist in our bodies or in those with whom we come into contact.

Unbelief is the cause of our powerlessness. If we truly believed and acted as if God's word was true our experience of the supernatural would be just that: supernatural.

Christians of the New Testament church believed and lived as if Jesus could return at any time. There is an urgent necessity for us to live in the same way as our Christian ancestors. There is a need to reawaken our expectation of God's promises.

Our beliefs can either be limiting to our spiritual growth, development and achievement or they can release us so that God is totally freed to give power to and prosper us. If we are struggling to break through in our prayer life, relationship with God, and answers to needs and spiritual growth, then one of the key areas to focus upon is what we actually believe. When all seems to go wrong around us, is our belief in God's promises holding firm and steady or are we wavering and tossed from 'pillar to post'?

> **Exodus 15:26**
> *If you will diligently hearken to the voice of the Lord your God, and do that which is right in his eyes, and give heed to his commandments and keep all his statutes, I will put none of the diseases upon you which I put upon the Egyptians; for I am the Lord, your healer.*

Conclusion

Revelation 19:7,8
Let us rejoice and exalt and give him the glory, for the marriage of the Lamb has come, and his Bride has made herself ready; it was granted her to be clothed with fine linen, bright and pure – for the fine linen is the righteous deeds of the saints.

During the course of this book we have discovered that as Gentile Christian believers we have generally missed the deeper significance and oozing richness of what the Bible writings actually contain. Much of this is because we do not fully understand the ceremonies, meaningful rituals, historic background of the Jewish people and most importantly, the symbols that God uses in scripture.

We do not connect the workings of God in and through the Jewish people because we do not understand them as God's chosen race. We often deal with certain terminology in the New Testament blindly. We do not always fully understand because they are tightly linked with Jewish culture and symbols that are often unknown to us.

Jewish people wrote the Old Testament. Much of the New Testament is not only a direct fulfillment of the Old Testament but it brings Gentiles into the same covenant promises. Jesus, of course, becomes the Lamb of God, and the cross wins a victory against Satan's power and influence. Another aspect is that most of the New Testament was faithfully written by three prominent Jewish people: John, Paul and Peter. These not only wrote for Jewish people but also for the Gentiles and the Christian Church. This is partly why we have a New Testament written in Koine Greek ('Koine' meaning the common language spoken at the time) and not Hebrew.

Paul proclaimed himself an apostle to the Gentiles by saying:

Romans 11:13,14
Now I am speaking to you Gentiles. Inasmuch then as I am an apostle to the Gentiles, I magnify my ministry in order to make my fellow Jews jealous, and thus save some of them.

Paul's ministry was to fulfill the precise commission of Jesus and preach the gospel to all nations. He was also stirring his fellow Jewish people to a jealousy that would cause them to recognize Yeshua as the Son of God and bring them to His Kingdom.

The roots of the Christian church are in God's chosen people, our Jewish friends. It is not acceptable for us as Gentile Christian believers to ignore, criticize or abandon our roots.

Paul explained this, saying:

Romans 11:17-21
If some of the branches were broken off, and you, a wild olive shoot, were grafted in their place to share the richness of the olive tree, do not boast over the branches. If you do boast, remember it is not you that support the root, but the root that supports you. You will say, 'Branches were broken off so that I might be grafted in'. That is true. They were broken off because of their unbelief, but you stand fast only through faith. So do not become proud, but stand in awe. For if God did not spare the natural branches, neither will he spare you.

The natural olive branches mentioned by Paul in this scripture refer to the Jewish people (who not only know their God-given place but take it very seriously) whilst the wild olive branches are the Gentiles, grafted in.

As Gentile believers we are clearly warned not to boast in our pride and arrogance. Our root is the same root as that of the Jewish people:

Romans 11:21,22
If God did not spare the natural branches, neither will he spare you. Note then the kindness and the severity of God; severity toward those who have fallen, but God's kindness to you, provided you continue in his kindness; otherwise you too will be cut off.

To help us understand this still further, let's take a look at the traditional process leading to a wedding.

Understand Jewish culture through the marriage ceremony

Why choose marriage as an example? The reason is quite simple. As we read both the Old and New Testaments, reference in one way or another is often made to an aspect of marriage. In truth, there are some significant parallels that we can learn between the old Jewish wedding culture and the Gentile Christian Church. Let's take a moment to discover what these links are.

As part of the old Jewish culture, a man who wanted to marry a woman would go to her father's house to speak with him about his intentions. The man would tell the father about who he is, what he does, how much he earns, what he can offer and how he intends to look after his daughter. If the father agrees that the man is suitable, the prospective groom agrees to pay him a sum of money. The amount of money offered demonstrates the love that the man has for the daughter. Therefore the greater the gift of money offered to the father the higher the love and value that the 'groom' signifies that he places upon his prospective wife.

When this agreement is complete the man walks to the room where his prospective wife is preparing a betrothal meal. He knocks on the door. If she opens the door it signifies that she has accepted the man's proposal. They then share the meal together and drink wine together. The drinking of this wine signifies that the betrothal is complete.

On completion of the betrothal a ceremonial bath and giving of gifts takes place. The woman uses the gifts to remind herself of him. But why is there a need to be reminded of her future husband? What happens next is the man goes away. He leaves his future bride to prepare a sort of honeymoon suite. This is usually an extension that is carefully built as part of his father's home.

People quite naturally ask the man, "When are you going to collect your bride?" The typical response to this question would be, "I don't know; only my father knows." The reason for this response is because it is up to the father to decide when he will give permission for his son to go and collect his bride.

When the time comes and permission to go is given to the son, this would typically be done at night. On arrival at the bride's home the man sounds a trumpet call. Her task is to be constantly expectant, ready and equipped for this moment and to go as soon as she is finally called.

The two then travel together to the home and prepared room of the future groom. Once there they spend seven days together in the room. On the eighth day they come out of the room, share in a wedding feast and marry.

Paul talked about the Christian wife and husband in his letter to the Ephesians. Wrapped up with his statements he compares the couple with the church (the bride or wife) and Jesus (the bridegroom or husband). John also says:

> **Revelation 19:9**
> *Blessed are those who are invited to the marriage supper of the Lamb.*

So what are the conclusions that we can make between the traditional Jewish wedding symbols and the Christian believer?

The marriage symbolism paralleled

THE PRICE OF LOVE

> **John 15:13**
> *Greater love has no man than this, that a man lay down his life for his friends.*

Jesus demonstrated before His Father how much He loves you and me. He willingly gave His life. He chose the exact moment of His own death. His act of love for us cost Him everything.

KNOCKING AT THE DOOR

> **Revelation 3:20**
> *Behold, I stand at the door and knock; if anyone hears my voice and opens the door, I will come in to him and eat with him, and he with me.*

The price has been totally paid, and now Jesus comes to knock at the door. The decision to answer the door is individually ours.

BETROTHAL COMPLETE

When the door has been opened we share in communion, the drinking of wine. What many do not fully appreciate is that participating in Holy Communion is effectively a betrothal of ourselves to Jesus. It is something that only those that are consecrated (set apart for God) participate in as part of their sanctification.

It is a very serious thing that we do when participating in Holy Communion, the Eucharist or whatever other term we may use. For this reason it is worth considering these words very carefully:

1 Corinthians 11:28-30
Let a man examine himself, and so eat of the bread and drink of the cup. For anyone who eats and drinks without discerning the body eats and drinks judgment upon himself. That is why many of you are weak and ill, and some have died.

I believe that this statement by Paul is clear and speaks for itself.

BAPTISM

The Christian's ceremonial bath is baptism, the receiving of the Holy Spirit and the gifts that are constantly used in memory of Jesus and to the glory of God until Jesus returns.

PREPARING A PLACE

Jesus said:

John 14:2,3
In my Father's house are many rooms, if it were not so, would I have told you that I go to prepare a place for you? And when I go and prepare a place for you, I will come again and will take you to myself, that where I am you may be also.

Jesus has gone, and so we as the church are now waiting for Him to return.

PREPARE FOR THE RAPTURE

Matthew 24:42
Watch therefore, for you do not know on what day your Lord is coming.

No one knows when Jesus will return, but one thing we do know is that we must be prepared, ready and watching for His coming. Just as the groom suddenly arrived outside the house of his bride with the blast of the trumpet so we read:

1 Thessalonians 4:16-17
The Lord himself will descend from heaven with a cry of command, with the archangel's call, and with the sound of the trumpet of God. [The church, the true believers] shall be caught up together with them in the clouds to meet the Lord in the air; and so we shall always be with the Lord.

Our role as Christian believers is to stay fully alert and constantly pressing forwards for more of God. There is no standing still in the believer's walk with God.

THE SEVEN DAYS

For seven days (the seven days of *huppah* – the canopy under which the marriage ceremony is performed) the bride and groom were 'locked' away in the room. The marriage was finally consummated.

The seven days mentioned here link with Daniel's seven-day (seven-year tribulation) prophecy. This appears to suggest that whilst the tribulation is taking place on earth the Church will be 'hidden' away.

What does it mean to be ready and prepared?

Jesus reminds us to be vigilant, saying:

Luke 12:35-40 (NIV)
Be dressed ready for service and keep your lamps burning, like servants waiting for their master to return from a wedding banquet, so that when he comes and knocks they can immediately open the door for him. It will be good for those servants whose master finds them watching when he comes. Truly I tell you, he will dress himself to serve, will have them recline at the table and will come and wait on them. It will be good for those servants whose master finds them ready, even if he comes in the middle of the night or toward daybreak. But understand this: If the owner of the house had known at what hour the thief was coming, he would not have let his house be broken into. You also must be ready, because the Son of Man will come at an hour when you do not expect him.

Only those who are firmly rooted and grounded in the word of God will endure to the end. We must spend daily time with God in prayer – read His word prayerfully and daily commit ourselves totally to Him.

We must prepare daily to meet our saviour.

Jude :17-25
But you must remember, beloved, the predictions of the apostles of our Lord Jesus Christ; they said to you, 'In the last time there

will be scoffers, following their own ungodly passions.' It is these who set up divisions, worldly people, devoid of the Spirit. But you, beloved, build yourselves up on your most holy faith; pray in the Holy Spirit; keep yourselves in the love of God; wait for the mercy of our Lord Jesus Christ unto eternal life. And convince some, who doubt; save some, by snatching them out of the fire; on some have mercy with fear, hating even the garment spotted by the flesh. Now to him who is able to keep you from falling and to present you without blemish before the presence of his glory with rejoicing, to the only God, our Saviour through Jesus Christ our Lord, be glory, majesty, dominion, and authority, before all time and now and for ever. Amen.

Bibliography[54]

Collins, W.; McLeod, W.T. (Editor); *The Collins Dictionary & Thesaurus in one volume;* William Collins & Sons, London & Glasgow [now HarperCollins] (1990)

Gager, John G.; *The Origins of Anti-Semitism,* OUP (1983)

Gosiewski, L.; *The Language of Knowing Our Heavenly Father's Heart and Will,* Onwards and Upwards Publishers (2012)

Hess, Tom; *Pray for the Peace Of Jerusalem. Until her salvation shines like a blazing torch,* Progressive Vision (2000)

Johnson, Paul; *A History of the Jews,* Harper Perennial (1987)

Kresge, Ted; *The Encyclopaedia Of Bible Prophecy: The Last Days (Three Volumes),* Armageddon Books (1999)

LaHaye, Tim; Hindson, Ed (Editors); *Exploring Bible Prophecy from Genesis to Revelation, Clarifying the meaning of every prophetic passage,* Harvest House (2011)

Milis, Joseph; *Jerusalem. The Illustrated History of the Holy City,* Carlton Publishing (2012)

Jones, Dr Timothy Paul, et al; *Rose Guide to End-Times Prophecy,* Rose Publishing (2011)

Renn, Stephen D.; *Expository Dictionary of Bible Words: Word Studies for Key English Bible Words Based on the Hebrew and Greek Text,* Hendrickson (2005)

Rausch, David; *A Legacy of Hatred. Why Christians Must Not Forget the Holocaust,* (1984)

Rycroft, Dr Haskell; *Who is Gog and where is Magog,* (2010)

---

[54] This bibliography has been specially included as a suggested tool to help readers study the topics covered in this book. Unless stated otherwise the author does not claim to have read or used these suggestions in the writing of this book.

Stormont, G.; *A Man Who Walked With God,* Harrison House (1989)

Tozer, A.W.; Bailey A.M. (Compilation); *Man. The Dwelling Place of God,* Christian Publications (1966)

Wigglesworth, S.; *Smith Wigglesworth Devotional,* Whitaker House (1999)

Wigglesworth, S.; *Greater Works,* Whitaker House (2000)

Useful Web Sites and Resources

The following resources will help those who wish to explore Hebrew and Greek origins or look for sources of information.

Blue Letter Bible
www.blueletterbible.org/Bible.cfm

Strong's Concordance with Hebrew and Greek Lexicon
www.eliyah.com/lexicon.html

Hebrew and Greek Lexicons – Bible study tools online
www.biblestudytools.com/lexicons

Wikipedia
en.wikipedia.org/wiki/Messiah_claimants

Contact the Author

To contact the author, please send an email to:

info@chasingyourdreams.co.uk
- or -
renewedlifehealingministries@gmail.com

Or connect with him on Facebook:

www.facebook.com/leon.gosiewski

More information about the author's ministry can be found online:

www.chasingyourdreams.co.uk

Appendix I: Replacement Theology [55] [56]

Before I launch into this question it should be appreciated that I am only briefly looking at replacement theology and not the root belief system (other than its historical setting) known as dispensationalism from which this theology derives.

Let's begin by looking at two key word definitions:

Dispensationalism

The word 'dispensation' when applied to theology refers to the order of life, time and events by God. Dispensationalists believe that there have been dispensations – or what are better known as administrations – including a time of freedom (in the Garden of Eden) through to government (after the flood), promise (the patriarchal promise) and grace, with others in between.

Put simply dispensationalism is a literal evangelical Bible interpretation that believes God has dealt with man in diverse ways by providing dissimilar tests and making different promises during different times, or administrations, of history.

To put this in another way and link the context of this book, one of the key beliefs of dispensationalism is that God's plans for the Jewish people is different from His plans for the Church.

As with many theological positions, dispensational beliefs have developed and refined over time. It is for this reason we sometimes hear of classical (often a period identified from the 1800's to the mid 1900's), revised or modified (mid 1900's to mid 1980's) and progressive (mid 1980's to present) dispensationalism. As one begins to trace the ups and downs of this theology there is no doubt that truth has occasionally mixed and become 'lost' with man's pride and a lack of godly love. In the extreme case this has been revealed in bouts of acrimony, separation, denial and even hatred.

Setting the less attractive aspects of this belief to one side, the question is: will the wholesale acceptance of this theological

---

[55] Formally known as supersessionism
[56] See page 111

conviction make any difference to the central messages of scripture? Without a doubt the answer is no. Will some of the arguments and way in which these are sometimes presented please God? Without a doubt the answer is yes.

Adding tags and titles such as dispensationalism with complicated words like supersessionism adds little of true and lasting worth. In this sense we have learned little from the Scribes, Pharisees and Sadducees. Please understand, I am not trying to criticize but rather to concentrate upon the Word in Spirit and truth.

Jesus said:

> Matthew 7:16
> *You will know them by their fruits.*

The test is what are the fruits? Paul reminds us that, for now:

> 1 Corinthians 13:12
> *We see in a mirror dimly, but then face to face. Now I know in part; then I shall understand fully, even as I have been fully understood.*

There is no substitute for prayerfully reading God's word and seeking guidance of the Holy Spirit.

This book seeks to redress some of the historical errors and misunderstandings between the Christian church and Jewish people. To this end the following scriptures highlight how God views all of mankind:

> Romans 10:12
> *There is no distinction between Jew and Greek; the same Lord is Lord of all and bestows his riches upon all who call upon him.*

> Galatians 3:28
> *There is neither Jew nor Greek, there is neither slave nor free, there is neither male nor female; for you are all one in Christ Jesus.*

> Colossians 3:11
> *There cannot be Greek and Jew, circumcised and uncircumcised, barbarian, Scythian, slave, free-man, but Christ is all, and in all.*

Supersessionism

This is also known as 'Fulfilment Theology' and more commonly today 'Replacement Theology'. It comes from the word 'supersede' and refers to the superseding or replacement of the old covenant (Mosaic Law) with the new covenant.

So what is replacement theology and where does it come from?

Put in very simple terms, replacement theology is a teaching that among other things states that under the new covenant the Church has replaced Israel in the plans and promises of God. Effectively this teaching erroneously says that Israel are no longer God's chosen people.

This teaching finds its foundations in the rise of the New Testament church after the day of Pentecost. The Pentecost event is sometimes interpreted as a focal point that separated the Church from the Jewish nation. This view looks for support to the new covenant introduced by Jesus that replaced the old covenant or Mosaic Law. Indeed, this point could seem to give credence to the theology. However, in truth it is an oversimplification because separation between the Church and the Jewish nation arose from religious and social differences. As soon as disagreements and misunderstandings arose the rift steadily grew wider. The slippery slide of a downward spiral began and the divide became more and more acrimonious. In extreme cases this led to anti-Semitism.

These dissensions are parallel examples of those the Church now finds itself engaged in. Denominational differences, beliefs and theologies have arisen. Some of these lead to fierce debate and even acrimony as one group argues their case against another.

The fact is the early Church had its roots in Jewish culture. Jesus himself was born Jewish and he taught in parallel with Hebraic writings. Indeed, Jesus states:

Matthew 5:17-18
Think not that I have come to abolish the Law and the Prophets; I have come not to abolish them but to fulfil them. For truly, I say to you, till heaven and earth pass away, not an iota, not a dot, will pass from the law until all is accomplished.

Furthermore, we should not forget our heritage and the fact that if Luke was not Jewish by birth (a point that has some debate), Jewish people wrote all but two books of the New Testament. The church was originally essentially Jewish. Jesus even stated:

John 4:22
Salvation is from the Jews.

It is not so much a question of replacement but rather extension and inclusion.

Under the scope of the new covenant what seems to be missed is that Jesus is the means of cleansing and salvation for all people. This promise was made:

Hebrews 8:8
The days will come, says the Lord, when I will establish a new covenant with the house of Israel and with the house of Judah.

Rather than a rift being established between the Church and the Jewish people there should be union.

Writers such as John Gager (1983)[57] explain that part of the rift between the Church and Jewish people actually arose from the accusation that they were murderers of Jesus. Promoters of this view came from Gentile Christian leaders such as Ignatius of Antioch (50-117 AD) and Tertullian (155-230 AD) thereby adding fuel to what was a growing separation. There is of course truth in the statement, but it was sin that took Jesus to the cross and in this sense we are no less guilty.

In 305 AD The Council of Elvira added further fuel to the fire and forbade Christian-Jewish relationships through connections such as marriage, observing the Sabbath and even sharing a meal together. This was then followed in 325 AD by the Council of Nicea changing the Jewish feast of first fruits and the resurrection to what we know today as Easter. By making this change the Council was declaring that the Church should have nothing in common with Jewish beliefs.

We even have arguments today about when dispensationalism was first introduced. Some say, although it was not used as a term, the sentiment came with the beliefs of the apostles, whilst others point to a much later origin. As we have discovered, if dispensationalism goes back to the apostles it has a murky past.

As a theological cult system we can pinpoint dispensationalism to an Anglo-Irish evangelist and Plymouth Brethren minister named John Nelson Darby (1800-1882) who is generally, but not exclusively, attributed with the title of being the father of modern dispensationalism.

---

[57] See bibliography.

Darby believed that there is a distinction between the Church and Jewish nation, a theory born out of his 'sudden' (or secret) rapture theory suggesting two second comings of Christ.

Using an analogy Paul spoke about an olive tree in Romans chapter eleven. In this discourse about Israel's future salvation we are clearly reminded that unbelief is like a natural branch (referring to the Jewish people) cut off from the tree. Faith represents the grafting of the wild olive tree (a reference to Gentiles) grafted to the tree.

It is not the place of the branch, especially the grafted branch, to boast its supremacy. It is the root that supports and feeds the branches. A grafted branch is only there by acceptance and becoming one with the tree.

We are all called to show love and honour to God and our neighbour, not contempt and hate. Joel reminds us of God's words:

Joel 3: 2 (NASB)
I will gather all the nations, and bring them down to the valley of Jehoshaphat. Then I will enter into judgment with them there on behalf of my people and my inheritance, Israel, whom they have scattered among the nations; and they have divided up my land.

It is an awesome thing to come against God and His chosen people.

Jewish people are very aware of their God-given identity as the Olive Tree and they take this seriously. Paul wrote these words:

Ephesians 2:12
Remember that you were at that time separated from Christ, alienated from the commonwealth of Israel, and strangers to the covenants of promise, having no hope and without God in the world.

How amazing that some within the Church today should consider themselves superior to and outside of the commonwealth of Israel, separating themselves from God's intended citizenship as fellow heirs with the Jewish people.

Appendix II: The Love Gospel [58]

The emphasis of the love gospel is upon God's benevolence and performing good and loving acts toward others in order to 'earn' the right to speak to them about Jesus.

Those that follow this trend will not speak of God's judgment, hell or Jesus as the only way, truth and life. They also avoid speaking about fearing God.

When leading people to Jesus, the need to repent and what this really means is not highlighted. The emphasis moves away from 'salvation from sin' and towards 'salvation from a tough life'. The message is that God loves and those that love God and give to Him will receive financial prosperity and health in return.

The overall context of scripture and the warnings of disobedience and unfaithfulness are not mentioned.

The 'love gospel' is a false gospel. Paul warned:

Acts 20:30
From among your own selves will arise men speaking perverse things, to draw away the disciples after them.

Taking this point further and speaking about the last days, John said:

1 John 2:18,19
Many antichrists have come; therefore we know that it is the last hour. They went out from us, but they were not of us

The increase of false messages and a watered down gospel and Bible teaching are all signs of the end and a heightened need for vigilance. Shockingly, many of these are coming from within the Church itself.

---

[58] See pages 29 and 74

Appendix III: Psalm 83 [59]

This is a Psalm of Asaph but who was Asaph?

As far as we can establish, Asaph (1020-920 BC) was King David's choirmaster or director of music. He conceivably wrote twelve Psalms (50,73-83) making him, if this is correct, more prolific than many of the 'minor' prophets, James and Peter.

Asaph was from a priestly Levite background, resident with his family in Jerusalem. His father was Berekiah, doorkeeper of the Ark, and his well-known brother was Zechariah. Indeed, following Zechariah's murder Asaph expressed his feelings in Psalm 73 where he admits to almost slipping from his faith.

Asaph lived through many upheavals including the rise and fall of Solomon and the division of the kingdom of Israel.

Psalm 83 is a two-part prayer. Verses 1-8 seek God's holy and perfect judgment on the enemies of Israel. Verses 9-18 move close to seeking the salvation of the enemies but call for God's vindication.

---

[59] See page 107

Other Books by the Author

The Language of Love, Forgiveness, Faith, Prayer and Healing
Onwards and Upwards Publishers

What is genuine love? Why does the church seem to lack God's power? Should we really expect God to answer all our prayers? Why are some people not healed? How do our words and actions towards others affect our personal wellbeing?

Tackling these and other difficult questions, the author invites us to join him on a journey of discovery into God's purposes for this generation. Opening up his heart, he shares broadly from his experiences, knowledge of the Bible and wisdom that he has gathered over the years. In doing so, the author and reader together explore the power of language – how our words affect the wellbeing and destinies both of ourselves and of those around us.

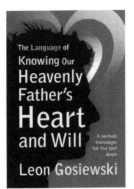

The Language of Knowing Our Heavenly Father's Heart and Will
Onwards and Upwards Publishers

Why are so many people leaving the church? Why are we largely bereft of God's power? If God is speaking, why are we not hearing? Is the Church in harmony with what the Bible teaches about it? Do we need revival?

Addressing these and other pertinent questions head on, the author unpacks what the scriptures have to say about knowing our heavenly Father, Jesus and the Holy Spirit on a relational level. Common misconceptions and unhelpful teachings are highlighted, and there is a call to return to a walk of holiness in which God is truly honoured as Lord and Saviour.